The Rob Lovett Fiore dei Liberi T… System

Primo…

Mark Lancaster
James Payton
Mark Berryman

Wyvern Media

Printed in Great Britain by
MPG Biddles Limited

ISBN 978 0 9564871 0 0

Published by
Wyvern Media
The Old Post Office
Quidenham
NR16 2AP
United Kingdom

Wyvern Media

Table of Contents

Introduction

Welcome to Primoris

This is the first part of a curriculum for training in a Western Martial Art based upon the historical system of Fiore dei Liberi.

Most people associate Martial Arts with the East - Karate, Kung Fu, etc. - but are totally unaware that the West, and in particular Europe, has a very rich martial heritage. In many ways this is understandable as Eastern based Martial Arts have captured the imagination of most people and the West has only tended to retain its martial heritage through sports such as boxing, wrestling and fencing.

Many Western based Arts have remained mostly dormant for hundreds of years, but are now coming back to the fore, due to the hard work of several leading Martial Artists and Martial Arts Schools. As these Arts are historic in nature they are often referred to as Historical European Martial Arts (HEMA) to distinguish them from the wider, yet encompassing, Western Martial Arts (WMA) that also include boxing, wrestling and other forms of Western based Arts.

In the early 1990s a new Martial Arts School was formed. As it was outside of the, then, expected Martial Arts community it was born with the name The Exiles. This new school solely focused on the Arts that had originated within Europe and in the late 1990s began to practise solely with the work of one late medieval Master - Fiore dei Liberi.

The system of Fiore dei Liberi covers a large area of combat from unarmed, through dagger and sword and onto pole arms and horse back combat. Rob Lovett, a founder of The Exiles and both lead interpreter and instructor, took the remaining work of Fiore dei Liberi and turned it into a living Martial Art with a structured curriculum. This curriculum moves students through several stages of training and this work covers that first stage. In acknowledgement of the historic background this work has been called "Primoris", or "First" in Latin.

One of the primary reasons for choosing the system of Fiore dei Liberi is that it is very complete. The large body of surviving work encompasses all the primary technical elements for someone to go into combat within the late medieval period. The system has the most effective and combat orientated principles that cover the main combat areas of:

- **Wrestling**
- **Dagger**
- **Short stick**
- **Sword with one hand**
- **Sword with two hands**
- **Spear and pole weapons**

Although it already contained a large amount of martial information, the system has required a large amount of work to turn it into a modern day Martial Art. This is not surprising as Fiore dei Liberi wrote his original manuscripts 600 years ago, for a readership that was already well versed in many of the martial principles that he built his system upon.

The result of all this hard work is that this is very much a living Martial Art and also an enjoyable subject for anyone interested in the medieval martial forms and weapon use.

Primoris is purely a training manual and is designed to be as user friendly as possible. To that end we have adhered to the following principles:

- **Simple** - The work is intended from beginning to end to be easy to follow. Theory and principles support techniques. References are made when detailing plays and drills to important principles that require focus.

- **Structure** - We have tried to keep the work as user friendly as possible, for example in the middle of practice you can make quick reference to parts of the book without being bogged down in masses of text and over complicated terminology and theory. Including only the items that are necessary at this stage, with drills and images taking the place of text in this work.

- **Practical** – The Exiles, as a whole, have a practical approach to the system we practise and it is vital that people can use the skills they are learning. We have not tried to fill this book with every conceivable topic and technique as it is easy to try and learn too much too quickly. Skills are constantly built upon and consolidated with drills and controlled sparring through consecutive levels. Primoris is a framework to move forward with.

Who Are We?

The authors of this work are all members of The Exiles. James Payton is a Graphic Designer by trade; Mark Berryman is a Senior Instructor of The Exiles and Mark Lancaster is an Instructor of The Exiles.

It has been our unenviable task to take the First Stage, Primoris, curriculum and turn it into a presentation that is understandable without direct instruction. Hopefully we have managed to achieve this; have done justice to the curriculum and have managed to impart the knowledge necessary for you to follow our training principles.

Although the Historical European Martial Arts community is comparatively small and new, it is a growing area within the wider Martial Arts community and this work is presented as a martial first-step to discovering a form of combat that existed and was used within Europe.

Your Study

Many Historical European Martial Arts publications concentrate on a reproduction and interpretation of the original source material. In themselves this will not teach the reader how to learn the Art, as they were originally written for a different audience who had contemporary knowledge and learning.

This work is different as our training programme gives students a grounding in Martial Arts and instruction that will allow them to develop smoothly through more complex and challenging martial techniques and concepts.

This work is different

The Exiles have spent many years building a complete system and developing a structured training programme. Our training programme gives students a grounding in Martial Arts and instruction that will allow them to develop smoothly through more complex and challenging martial techniques and concepts.

By using this work you are entering into a subject that is satisfying, martially complete, challenging and rewarding and you will learn a system with modern applications.

Master Fiore dei Liberi

Fiore dei Liberi came from the Friuli region of Northern Italy and was a fencing and combat master from the latter years of the 14c into the early 15c. Like many Masters of this period he tended to be selective in the people he taught and would not share his system with other masters, some of whom did challenge him to several duels which he won.

Many of his students were famous fighters of the time and others were nobles, minor nobles and despot leaders. His students went on to show the skill of his teaching by winning formal combat fights within tourney.

Fiore was obviously a learned man as he was able to read, write and draw. He also studied his Martial Art for over 40 years, which shows that he was either very lucky to have such a long life span for the period or he was used to a healthy general lifestyle.

At an early age Fiore was naturally attracted to the fighting arts and so spent many years learning the arts of unarmed, dagger, sword, spear and mounted fighting. He studied under both German and Italian masters, travelling far and wide, until he was recognised as a Master himself.

Fiore became very scornful of others who called themselves Master, stating that out of thousands of so-called Masters that only four could call themselves scholars and of those four scholars only one was truly a Master. This gives us a combat Master that studied hard for many years and developed a system that was both proven and effective.

So, how do we know all this? There are surviving manuscripts that describe the complete system of Fiore. His introductions give us a wealth of information on places and individuals that can be independently verified. The bulk of the manuscripts are, however, on fighting techniques and principles.

Between the manuscripts we have over 600 illustrations and over 26,000 words. Although much is repeated between the manuscripts they support each other and introduce new concepts, techniques and information that allow us to build a complete picture of this vast martial system.

The combined, surviving, work of Fiore dei Liberi presents us with the most detailed and informative historical Martial Art available to the modern martial artist.

Starting Primoris

Now we will start your Primoris training. Please take particular note of all the fundamentals that are contained within this work before you actually start training. It is very tempting to just go straight into the techniques and drills, but your training will be a lot more enjoyable and fulfilling if you use the entire programme.

Take your time and do not be afraid to ask questions. We provide a list of resources which includes on-line forums for this community and there is a lot of help and advice available. You can, of course, contact The Exiles directly and we will try and assist.

You are now ready to start learning a new Martial Art

Fundamentals Introduction

Although Primoris is about the principles of this Art, there are some fundamentals that need to be covered and learned at the very start. Without fundamentals you cannot build your skills correctly and will only learn a snap-shot Martial Art. For some people this can work, especially if they have innate abilities, but everyone benefits from basic skills that will enhance their natural and learned abilities.

Any form of serious training requires Health and Safety. It allows for the building of intensity within the training programme, which in turn builds up the skills that are practised within training. Only egotists will completely reject Health and Safety as being at the very base of any Martial Art; those who follow the principles of Health and Safety will experience benefits when training with fellow students.

To this we add basic Footwork, Turning and Falling within Primoris as these are core skills that are required throughout the system. Each section will introduce the key skills for the weapon or techniques being employed, but here you will be shown the basic knowledge that is required at this level of training.

Health and Safety

The reasons for having a clear set of Health and Safety rules are obvious. It is important that everyone is aware of a common set of rules to work from so that safety is always the first consideration. The following should be the very first thing any new student to a class learns.

Before any training takes place:

- The instructor should be made aware of any medical conditions or injuries that may affect a student's practice.

- It is the student's responsibility to ensure that any new injury is noted with the instructor on a regular basis.

- Consulting a physician where necessary is always the responsibility of the student.

- If a student takes part in training, then they are acknowledging their health and fitness to be of an appropriate level.

You should keep track of all injuries within an Accident Book. This can be a simple lined book for recording the date and time of any injuries. Such an approach can help to protect the instructor as well as giving information on the types of injuries that are being carried by students.

Health and Safety

'Stop'
Students should all be aware that should they hear (or even think they hear) the word 'stop' from anybody in the room they are to immediately do so, even if they are in mid-action, as long as the action of stopping is safe.

Stop should be called any time an instructor or observer sees something that may be unsafe, for example, if two people are drilling or sparring and there is an unsafe element like an arm lock being applied that the observer feels may be dangerous.

Tapping out
If, for example, you are being choked or doing some ground work it may not be possible to ask your opponent to stop when you are reaching your limit, in this case you should 'tap out'.

A tap out is simply that, tapping on your opponent with your hand before you take an injury. Students should practise tapping out so that they are aware of its meaning

Also, remember to always be aware of your opponent tapping on you!

Jewellery
Ideally, you should not allow jewellery within training as it can cause injury to both the wearer and other students. Should for any reason a person have on jewellery that cannot be removed then, as long as it causes no direct risk to other people, it can be worn at the person's own risk. If there is a risk to others it must be removed.

Pulling strikes
When either you or your opponent are learning something new, it is important to be prepared to 'pull' a strike, be it with your fist or a weapon.

You should not commit fully to a strike until both parties are comfortable with what is being covered, so that you are ready to pull the strike either by stopping it or changing the direction to avoid hitting your opponent.

'Harder'
Ultimately, to practise realistically, strikes must be made with power. You may find it easier when drilling or practising a technique, to start gently and build the power in response to your partner asking you to go harder. In this way, the person taking the strike is dictating the power they are comfortable with.

If in doubt step out
Should you ever be confused in a drill or a technique do not simply just stop, and rely on your opponent to pull the blow, you should either aim to put up some form of defence, or step back, well clear of any strikes. **Remember you can always say 'stop'.**

Fingernails
Fingernails must always be kept short for training.

Health and Safety

Safe training requires good, effective, equipment. With Primoris the list is not too exhaustive and will be affordable to any serious practitioner. Higher training levels require additional equipment, but this can be added as the skills and intensity of training increase.

The basic list of required equipment is:

Clothing

Clothing should be comfortable and durable, such as a T-shirt and cargo pants. Footwear can be normal training shoes, but ideally should be flat soled – such as boxing or wrestling boots. Flat soled footwear allows for the better use of the footwork within the system and helps to encourage the wearer to place their weight onto the front of the foot.

If you wish to have more expensive clothing then this is your choice, but remember that this system is built upon the medieval original and so you should be looking for clothing with comparable qualities – for example a T-shirt is light and similar to a medieval shirt. Flat, leather soled, medieval style boots or shoes are ideal for the footwork within the system.

Head Protection

It is important that you have adequate head protection for training.

With unarmed striking and wrestling you should look for a padded head guard. These are affordable and will allow for full contact strikes during unarmed training. It is recommended that you include the face grill protection as well, but this is your own choice.

Padded head guards are available from all main stream Martial Arts shops.

For sword use you must find head protection that fully protects the face, such as a high quality 1600N fencing mask. With a fencing mask it is advised that you also add the "coaching" padded protection for the top and sides of the mask. Additional padding and rear protection is also highly recommended.

There are specialist masks available and, although more expensive, these are fully recommended.

Health and Safety

Hand Protection

Hand protection fulfils two important roles – protecting you own hands and protecting your training partner. There is little point in having good hand protection if it will damage or hurt your opponent – for example you should not grapple with metal gauntlets!

For unarmed striking and drills fingerless sparing gloves (such as Martial Arts MMA gloves) are ideal as they allow for grappling and striking. These gloves will offer your hands protection, whilst reducing the impact of your blows against your training partner. They are very good in combination with padded head guards.

For sword training you will require gloves or leather gauntlets that cover the entire hand. Different people prefer different types of gloves and you can normally get something that will easily fit your budget – such as fencing gauntlets, cricket gloves, field hockey gloves, ice hockey gloves, etc. As well as protecting the top of the hands and fingers you should look for a glove that will give protection to the sides of the index and little fingers as these are often hit during sword play.

Padded Protection

In Primoris padded protection is not totally necessary as long as restraint is used, but it is still advised that you invest in good protection as the intensity of training levels increase.

There are numerous forms of body protection available for purchase – such as a fencing coaching leather plastron. If you choose modern protection then you should look for the highest quality available that allows flexibility in movement. Protection for sword work requires both movement and padding.

Traditional protection is also available from a vast range of suppliers. Again, remember that you will need to balance movement and protection and it is recommended that you have such items made to measure.

Any area that is likely to be hit with a sword cut or thrust must have adequate protection – particularly non-muscled bone and soft tissue areas. Always remember, though, that protection is never a substitute for good training and technique.

Health and Safety

Training Daggers

For training you need a rondel simulator – or waster. The rondel dagger was typically not sharp on the edge, but a pointed stabbing weapon. Due to this any wooden waster is more than adequate for training. The rondel waster should, ideally, be long enough reach to your elbow when gripped in the hand.

Using a wooden waster is much less dangerous than a metal weapon and at this level of training wood should only be used.

Training Swords

All swords used are of the hand-and-half, or longsword, variety. Within Oakeshott's classification system this would be a Type XVa. The hand-and-half is a sword that can be used both one handed and two handed. Specific designs are down to personal preference, but generally having a "scent-bottle" pommel is most suitable to training.

Wooden training swords (wasters) are available at relatively low cost and are good initial weapons.

The main problem with wooden wasters is that they do not flex. They also offer a false sense of security with regard to the damage they can inflict when compared to a metal sword. It should always be remembered that a wooden waster impacting at speed can inflict serious injury and so should be treated with the same amount of respect and control as a metal sword.

Rebated blunt metal swords are the ideal weapon for training. This is because good examples incorporate the weight, balance and flexibility of the original sharp sword. There is a good range of rebated steel and aluminium training wasters available in a variety of costs. The more expensive examples tend to be better and more durable.

Nylon and Plastic sword wasters are now becoming available as a functional alternative to both wood and steel as realistic training weapons.

Health and Safety

Equipment Maintenance

Whatever equipment you decide upon you must keep it properly maintained. Metal weapons must have burs removed and wooden weapons should be inspected for splinters. If a weapon shows signs of fracturing then it must be discarded. You must think about your training partner and ensure that your weapon will not cause any unforeseen damage.

Your own clothing and protection should also be maintained to ensure that it still provides the maximum protection and does not have any problems like ripping or fraying.

First Aid and Insurance

As well as good maintenance of equipment you must also ensure that you are covering other aspects of Health and Safety. An adequate First Aid kit should be available during all training sessions. Many sports First Aid kits are available for direct purchase and tend to include all of the items that you are likely to need. Please remember that it is normally illegal to dispense medicines – for example for pain relief and you should seek First Aid Training. An Accident Book should also be kept so that all injuries, accidents and incidents can be properly recorded.

It is highly recommended that you also seek insurance cover – for both yourself and training partners. Personal Accident and Public Liability should be the minimum level of insurance that you are looking for and discuss the policy with the provider and let them know exactly the nature of training that you will be undertaking.

Official Equipment

As you build up your equipment list and increase your training you will settle on your own, approved, official equipment and will wish to expand upon the range.

For example, we have an official wrestling Jack (combat jacket) that was specifically designed to stay within the system yet allow us consistency across our training. In addition we have soft training clothes that gives us both a uniform look and a good standard for students.

Fiore's Principles

From the original manuscripts Fiore dei Liberi shows us a lot of martial principles and gives us a lot of information. Although presented in a form that was more familiar to a medieval reader they are fully understandable to the modern reader with a little bit of guidance.

Within Primoris we introduce several of these principles and, although they were laid down six hundred years ago, they still apply to the modern day practise of this Martial Art.

In common with our own society, the later medieval society used symbology to quickly show ideas in a visual form. One of the greatest forms of illustration used by Fiore dei Liberi is known as the Segno. Here we present the Segno and describe its significance, as it will form part of the foundation behind the entire Art.

Fiore's Principles

The segno, to give its common name, summarises the martial principles of Fiore in a single presentation.

The figure has the crown of the Master above his head, showing that these are the true principles of knowledge that need to be obtained.

Seven swords are shown, each showing a different one of the colpi (blows) used within the system. Note that these can also apply to non-sword strikes:

- **Two downward colpi – called Fendente – one from each side**
- **Two horizontal colpi – called Mezani – one from each side**
- **Two upward colpi – called Sottani – one from each side**
- **A single thrusting colpi – called Punte**

Ironically the paths shown by these colpi are not totally correct, but used as a principle representation of the colpi. We will see what Fiore says about individual colpi in the specific cutting section of this book.

Fiore's Principles

The Segno also shows four animals which embody Fiore's main principles of the martial system:

Lynx with Compass

This is above the Master's head with the word "Advisement" and shows the necessity of good vision, or judgement, which is a medieval trait of the Lynx together with the compass to measure distance and timing.

Tiger with Arrow

The tiger, on the left, represents quickness and speed and states that the arrow will not overtake him.

Lion with Heart

The Heart is a well known virtue of the Lion and represents daring and courage that invites combat with others.

Elephant and Castle

The Castle, upon the Elephant, is taken from the Indian Howdah and shows that all strong fighting is done from the legs and feet – i.e. good solid footwork. In medieval bestiaries they believed that the Elephant could not bend it's knees and so would never willingly go to the ground as it would not be able to get back up again. This is born out in medieval systems which do not represent any ground fighting, suggesting that it was not considered a good idea to allow yourself to be put on the ground, even though you should bend your knees.

Principles of the Segno

We can see from this simple diagram that Fiore is representing the martial principles that a Master must know his lines of attack together with judgement of time and distance; speed and quickness; courage and daring; and the ability to fight from a strong footwork base without going to ground.

Abrazare Principles

For the unarmed, Abrazare, Fiore gives us several principles that apply within unarmed fighting and throughout the system. These are:

- **Strength**
- **Speed**
- **Knowledge of Binds**
- **Knowledge of Locks**
- **Knowledge of Breaks and Dislocations**
- **Strikes to Vulnerable places – namely the eyes; the nose, the soft areas under the chin and the flanks**
- **Knowledge of Throws**

Fiore's Masters

Fiore's manuscripts include some very simple yet effective, symbolic methods of conveying information and detail. One of these methods is by using what Fiore calls "Masters". Masters can be looked at as experts in different parts of the system and are utilised throughout the illustrations, with their students, to indicate how a particular technique is used and achieved.

We do not follow the same symbology within Primoris, but we do follow the same principles. The use of the word "Master" should not be looked upon as a negative term, as some modern uses of the word might imply, but rather as mastery of a skill and various applications of that skill.

To this end it is very important that you grasp the use of the Master as it will quickly allow you to understand the intended application of techniques and the described principles.

Fiore's Masters

It is important, whilst reading this book, to understand how Fiore utilises his concept of Masters, so this section will give details of how these are used.

The first time that Fiore introduces us to the Masters is in the stages of a fight. He states that the first Master we will encounter is "Master Battle". This Master knows how to fight - cut, thrust, keep distance, timing, etc. The Master Battle is an expert at the main fight itself.

As Master of Battle engages in a fight he will either win his attack, withdraw to re-enage or reach a point that his opponent can turn on him with a counter technique.

These counter techniques are not the same as blocking or defending against an attack by Master Battle, but are much more skilled. They are where the opponent can vanquish Master of Battle with a fully skilled counter.

Fiore calls this first counter a "Remedy" and this introduces the next Master. Master Remedy is more skilled than Master of Battle as he knows all of the same techniques and how to counter many of them with his own. The majority of Fiore's recorded work shows Master Remedy - probably because of lot of people at the time were already competent fighters, close to the Master Battle stage, and Fiore was showing how to win a fight.

It is possible to counter Master Remedy and Fiore now shows us "Master Contra". In reality this is where someone attacks as Master Battle, his opponent uses skill to counter as Master Remedy and then the original attacker knows how to counter this with a new technique and becomes Master Contra.

Finally, Fiore does mention a fourth "Master Contra-Contrary", but this is rarely illustrated. This Master is the counter of the counter to the counter of the original attack! Fiore does state that an encounter will not go beyond the rare Master Contra-Contrary, which is obvious as at the end of a four technique encounters the combatants will either have withdrawn to re-engage or one will have lost the fight.

Taking an example of the complete Master encounter, we would have:

1. **Combatant 1 attacks as Master of Battle**
2. **Combatant 2 counters as Master Remedy**
3. **Combatant 1 counters as Master Contra**
4. **Combatant 2 counters as Master Contra-Contrary**

The number of options, techniques and moves available to each master reduces dramatically through the encounter and, in reality, most fights are at the Master Battle to Master Remedy stage.

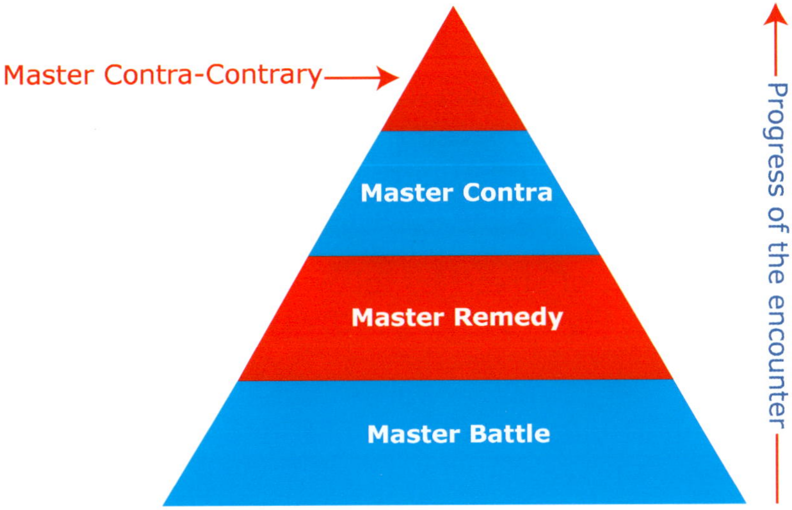

The concept of Masters is also used by Fiore to show the areas where a student needs to become expert. For example the following are four Masters of Dagger from one of the manuscripts:

Each in turn shows a different expertise of Dagger combat – disarming, breaks, locks and mastery of unarmed. Also note, though, that each illustration shows an older Master, indicating that more experience is required for each level of mastery.

Within the illustrative combat techniques of the Manuscripts Fiore starts each section with the primary Master Remedy – for example the Master at countering a dagger using his left hand. Once the Master has shown the main technique then he "passes" control over to a student, or scholar, in the illustrations to show the other techniques within that section.

Warm-up

Warming up is essential before starting any exercise or physical activity to avoid injury and prepare the body and mind for increased physical workload and stresses. Always perform a warm-up before starting a training session, a warm-up needs to consist of stretches followed by a gradual increase in intensity in physical activity.

It is very easy to ignore having a warm-up before training, but it is important that you do not ignore warming up. Without a decent warm-up your body will not be fully ready for the activities of training and although it may not seem to affect you during that training it could well have a built up affect over time that leads to continued complaints and injuries.

Within a training session you are much more likely to cause a strain to your muscles if you have not fully warmed up.

You want to get the most out of training and to do this it is necessary to treat your body properly.

Warm-up

Stretching

In Martial Arts and other strenuous activities, the muscles and joints of the body can be pushed and flexed beyond their everyday range of motion and also used more vigorously. A good stretch is important to prepare your muscles and joints to avoid pulls and tears.

The following is a basic set of stretches to target the major areas of the body and is the minimum you should be aiming to do. Individuals with any problem areas may want to add in additional stretches to target these areas. These stretches take 7 to 10 minutes and will be followed by light cardiovascular warm-up.

Start with the top of the body and work your way down to make it easier to remember the order of your stretches.

Neck *– 30 seconds of stretching*
The neck takes a lot of stress in Martial Arts, especially with throws, strikes and grappling.

- Roll the head forwards and backwards working up to the maximum range of motion in these directions.
- Roll the head from left to right working up to the maximum range of motion in these directions.
- Move your head around in a circular motion

Warm-up

Shoulders *– 90 seconds of stretching*
The shoulders are made up of several different muscles and these stretches target them in different ways.

With your arms raised straight out from your sides make slow small circles rotating your arms forward. Make the circles bigger until you are using the full range of motion in your arms. Then rotate them the opposite way in steadily smaller circles back to your starting position.

Raise an arm over your head and try to place the palm of your hand onto your upper back, use your free arm to apply pressure to the elbow to stretch the shoulder out, slowly apply more pressure for about 15 seconds and then change arms.

Warm-up

Place an arm across the front of your body, trying to touch the inside of your elbow to the opposite shoulder. Use your free hand to apply pressure to the arm and the stretch. Hold for about 15 seconds and change arms.

Chest, *Arms and Shoulders – 2 minutes*
5 sets of maximum repetition push-ups up to a maximum of 15 push-ups per set. Keep your back straight and elbows tucked in by your sides. Perform the push-ups from the knees if you find it too difficult to do them from your feet.

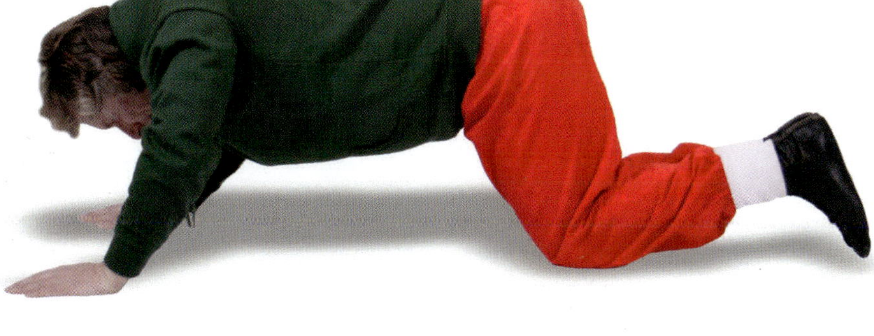

Warm-up

Abdominals – *90 seconds*
The abdominal muscles are used more than most would expect in Martial Arts, as they are involved in all of the motions of the upper body.

Lying on your back and with your knees raised and feet crossed perform 5 sets of maximum repetition crunches. To a maximum of 20 crunches per set.

Lower back – *1 minute*
With your legs stretched wide apart try to touch your left foot with your right hand then swing to touch your right foot with your left hand, alternating between to two. Try and keep your arms straight so you are using the rotation of your back and body to bring your hands to your feet.

Warm-up

Legs *– 2 minutes 40 seconds*

Standing up straight, hold your right foot to your buttock with both of your hands holding it in place and keeping your knees together. After about 10 seconds change feet. Repeat this twice.

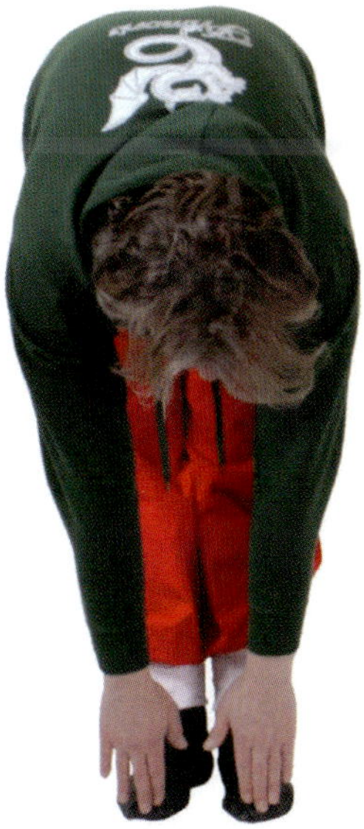

With both legs straight reach to touch your toes and hold for 15 seconds, repeat this 4 times pushing a little further as you do. If you are very flexible, touch the floor and if your not so flexible go as far down your legs as you can.

Make small circles with your feet, stretching them in all directions particularly pointing your toes upwards towards the knees.

Warm-up

Cardiovascular Warm-up

Similarly to stretching, a cardiovascular element should be included as part of a warm-up after stretches. A few minutes of moderate activity is all that is required to get the blood flowing to the muscles and the heart rate up in readiness for further activity. You can do any of the following example for 3 to 5 minutes, a combination of them or anything else that gets your heart rate up.

- Skipping
- Jogging (on the spot if necessary)
- Striking on focus mitts or a punch bag
- Perform push ups and after each one get onto your feet and jump as high as you can twice followed by 5 star jumps before doing another push up and so on.

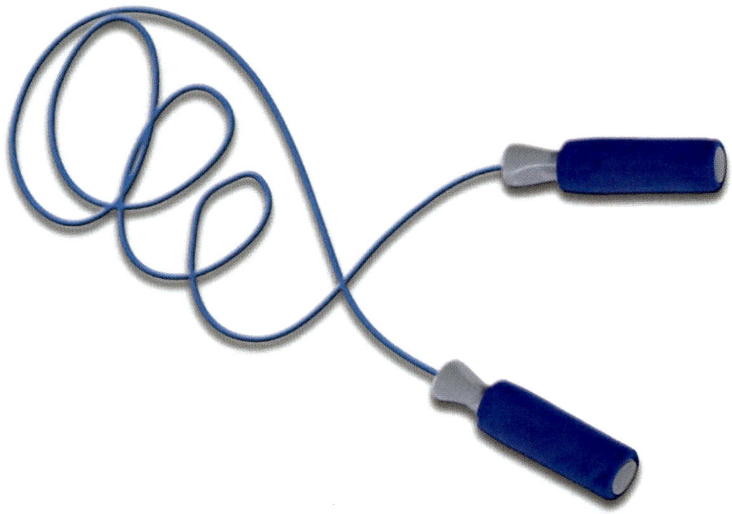

Cool - down

Cooling down helps to prevent sore muscles and joints by getting rid of the Lactic Acid build up in the muscles during intense activity. After a training session, you may have been using your muscles close to full power and this causes micro tears in the muscle fibres which then leads to soreness.

To cool down, follow a stretch routine like the one outlined for warming up. Cooling down does not need to be followed by any kind of major cardiovascular activity, but a light jog on the spot or some skipping can help to flush out the muscles and relax and muscles or joints that have seen major stress. If you are going to include some kind of light cardiovascular in your cool-down, do it before your cool-down stretch off.

Hydration

Proper hydration is vital for training. Ensure you drink plenty of liquids before training but not any large amounts an hour or so before your session. During your session, sip your drink every 5-10 minutes. Do not gulp large amounts down and after training drink plenty to help re-hydrate your body.

Footwork and Turning

There are different forms of footwork within the Fiore system, but at the Primoris level we formally concentrate on one important aspect, called the Accrease, and three forms of footwork that involve a turn of the body – Mezza Volta, Tutta Volta and Volta Stabile.

All Martial Arts require good footwork as a foundation. People fight from the feet, both for power and for placement. The Fiore system is no different and includes footwork to pass one foot past another; increase or decrease a foot position; turn on the feet, adjust the feet, etc.

Closely associated with footwork, the Fiore system includes turns of the body, called Volta. These turns do require footwork but also alter the aspect of the body and, hence, the martial options and potential applications.

The importance of footwork was such that Fiore illustrated it within his Segno. This clearly shows that the fight is from the legs.

At this stage of training we present one main aspect of footwork - the Accrease - and show how this can be used with the three Volta turns.

It is important, though, that you follow your own body and find your own balance. By doing this you will naturally start to find out how to decrease, pass, find situations where you can Volta without the Accrease, etc. All of these aspects are covered in later training levels.

Accrease

Foot adjustment

The key to exploiting the effective use of the three Volta footwork turns within the system is the Accrease. This is not a strict increase or a decrease of the feet, but an adjustment of foot position which may be forwards, sideways or at an angle. Although forwards sounds like increase this is an adjustment and not a large step.

The Accrease adjustment is important for changing the angle of the foot and, hence, the direction of movement. Another important use is to clear one foot out of the way of the other for a step or to give initial power and momentum to a turn.

The Accrease is always used with the three Volta turns within the Primoris training level.

In defence the Accrease, without any additional footwork or turning, will also give a small vital measure of distance. This distance is often enough to create a cover, exchange, beat, etc. without losing the timing or alignment of an immediate counter strike.

Here are some examples

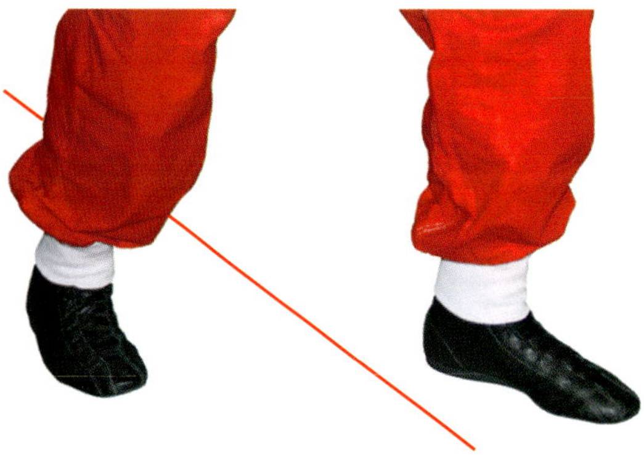

Starting Position

Here we have a normal left foot lead starting position. The position could also start with a right foot lead, in which case the Accrease works in the opposite. ▲

Example 1

Here the Accrease is made with the front left foot off to the left, clearing space for the rear right foot to come forwards or to make distance. ▲

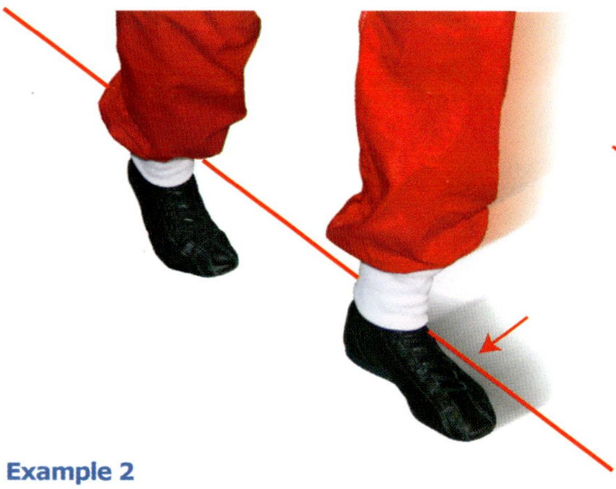

Example 2

The Accrease is made with the front left foot across the rear right foot. ▲

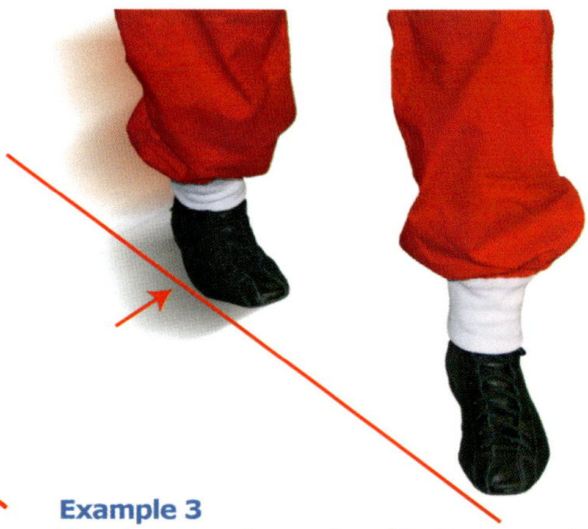

Example 3

The Accrease is made with the rear right foot across the front left foot. ▲

Mezza Volta

Half Turn

This footwork is called a Mezza Volta, or half-turn. It is a half-turn as the body is turned from one side, or half, to the other with the step. This is the natural attack and defence step.

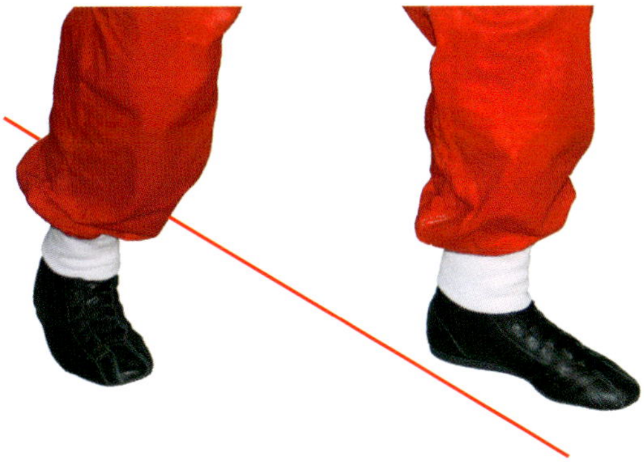

This is a left foot forward starting position. The centre of gravity is nicely balanced in the middle without the weight being mainly on the front or back foot. ▲

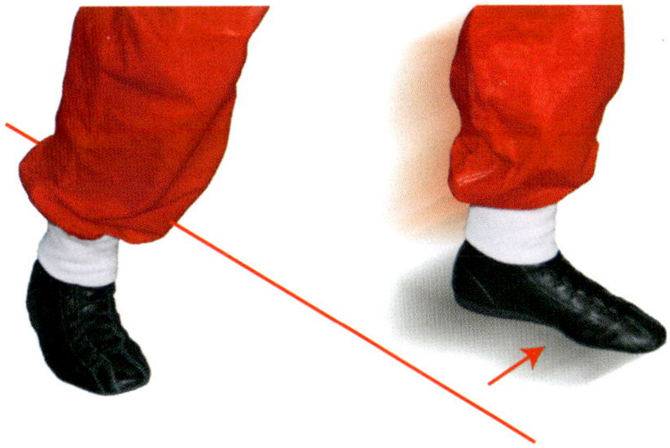

A small quick side step is taken with the front left foot out of the way to the left. This is called an Accrease. ▲

With the front foot out of the way, a step forward can now be made bringing the right foot to the front. ▲

The aim of the Mezza Volta is to make a quick step whilst keeping the balance of the body. The Mezza Volta can be made with either foot forward – for a right foot lead the Accrease is made to the right – and can be made forwards or backwards.

The Accrease is used as a small, quick, foot adjustment. It simply clears the way for the rear foot whilst maintaining the best balance through the entire step.

Tutta Volta

Complete Turn

The Tutta Volta is a full turn. It is used to turn the body to a different direction and is powered by the legs and hips. It is excellent for close encounters, such as throws and grappling.

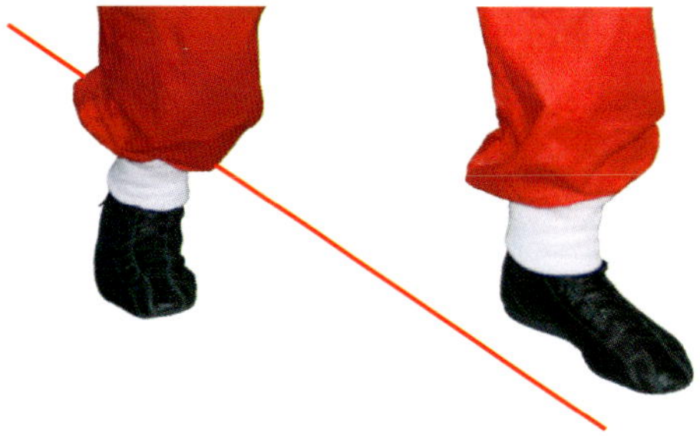

Here we have a left foot forward starting position, although this could equally be started in a right foot forward position. The centre of gravity is nicely balanced in the middle. ▲

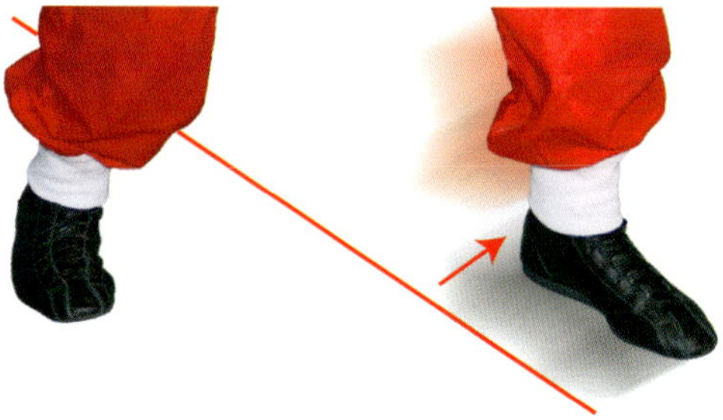

A small quick side step is taken with the front left foot out of the way to the left. This is called an Accrease. ▲

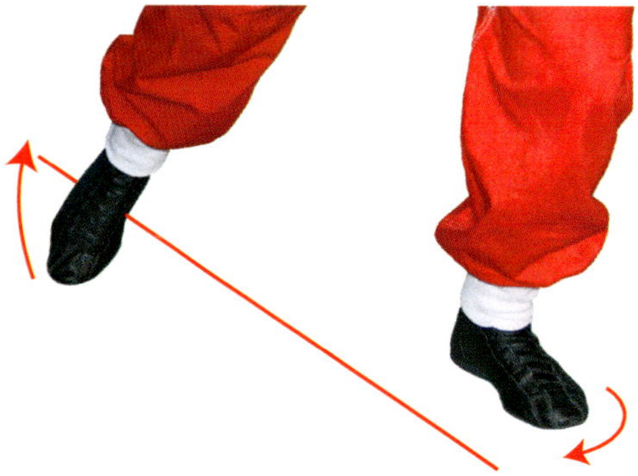

The Accrease powers a turn on the ball of the left foot. The right foot rotates around in a clockwise motion. It is important that the rotation with the right foot is with an extended leg rather than a basic step-through to give the turn energy. ▲

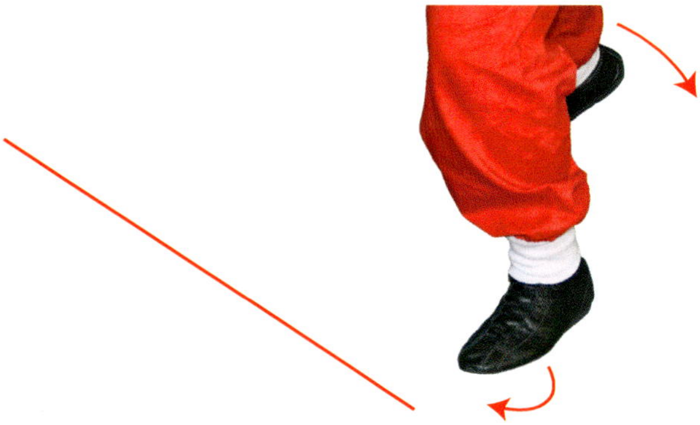

Here we are half way through the turn. The rotation is on the ball of the left foot with the right leg extended. ▲

Finally the turn is completed. This can be up to 180 degrees depending upon the situation. ▲

The Tutta Volta is a rotating turn that has a lot of speed and power. The speed of the turn is essential as there is only one point of contact with the ground during the actual turn, which means you can be over-balanced whilst turning. The Accrease is important as a small, quick, foot step as it applies momentum and direction.

The Tutta Volta can be achieved with either leg leading – left foot leading turns being done clockwise and right foot leading turns being done anti-clockwise.

Volta Stabile Rear

Stable turn from the rear foot

The Volta Stabile is a stable turn and is normally, at this level made with an Accrease adjustment of rear foot. The turn is stable because it maintains full contact with the ground for the actual turn and this is an excellent turn for grappling and dagger.

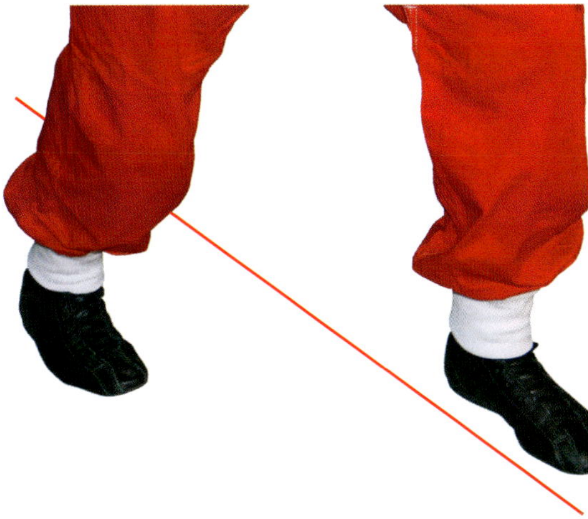

We have a left foot lead starting position with the centre of gravity nicely balanced in the middle of the stance. ▲

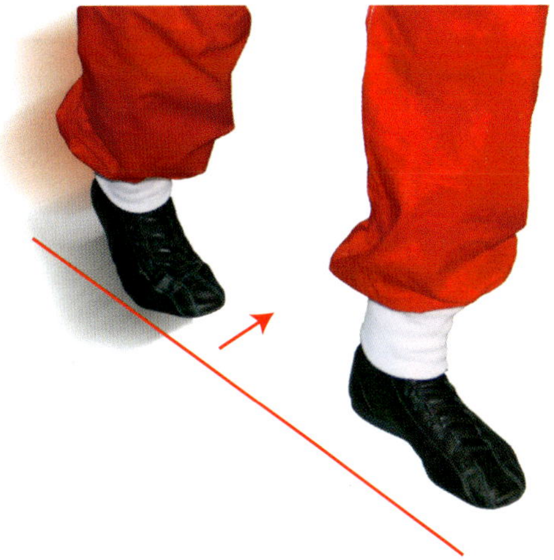

A quick Accrease of the rear right foot is made to the side of the left foot. This has to be quick as it is unstable at this stage of training. Later improvements will show how this can be more stable. ▲

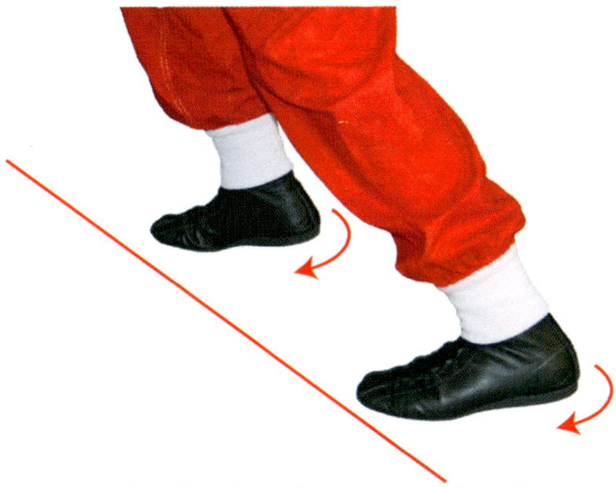

Immediately after the Accrease has been made the body is turned in a clockwise direction on the balls of both feet. This turns the body around completely. ▲

The Volta Stabile is a rotation of the entire body on both feet. The quick Accrease will give momentum and clear the rear foot out of the way - otherwise the legs would end up crossed on a complete turn. As both legs are involved in the actual turn this is also a very powerful piece of footwork.

The turn can be made with either foot leading. For a right foot lead the Accrease would be made with the trailing left to the right and the turn would be anti-clockwise.

Volta Stabile Front

Alternative stable turn from the front foot

It is also possible to perform the Volta Stabile, or stable turn, with an Accrease adjustment of the front foot. This alternative may be used to maintain distance or when in close grappling or contact situations. Again this turn is stable because it maintains full contact with the ground during the actual turn.

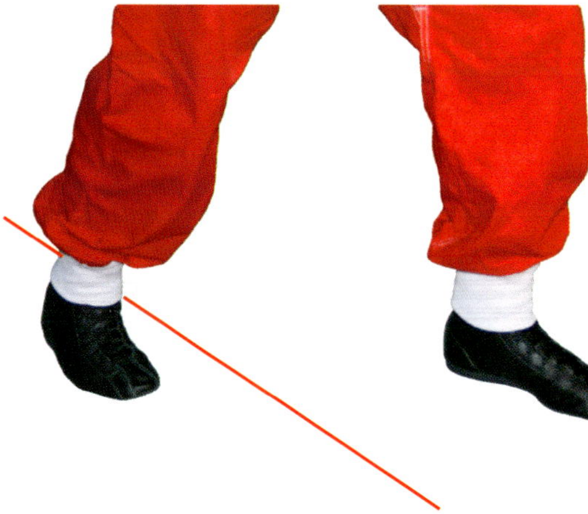

We have a left foot lead starting position with the centre of gravity nicely balanced in the middle of the stance. ▲

The Accrease adjustment is made with the front left foot coming quickly across the rear right foot. ▲

Immediately after the Accrease has been made the body is turned in a clockwise direction on the balls of both feet. This turns the body around completely. ▲

This variation of the Volta Stabile is very similar mechanically to the rear foot Volta Stabile. Apart from the obvious difference of the front foot being used for the Accrease. It also takes the body slightly to the right with the turn, rather than slightly to the left with the rear foot turn. Depending upon the martial situation this can have an advantage and so should also be practised.

As with the rear foot Volta Stabile, this version can also be done with a right foot lead, where the right foot Accreases across the front of the rear left foot and immediately followed by an anti-clockwise turn.

Falling and Break Falling

Knowing how to fall safely is an important aspect of combat. Although with this system we do not aim to fight on the ground, it is important for both training and for combat that if you are put to ground you learn to minimise this impact to your body and, where possible, be in a place to carry on the fight from a prepared position.

For training purposes you want to practise falling using suitable mats. If you do not have these available then it is worth booking facilities that do have them available so that you can fully practise your falling.

As you become more comfortable with correctly falling you will be able to move to practising light falls on any soft ground, but you should not be tempted to practise on a solid surface. Remember that falling will always hurt and the purpose of learning how to fall is to minimise that hurt and any potential injuries.

Falling must be properly learned before you move onto any of the throws within the system. If you do not know how to fall then you cannot be thrown with any degree of safety.

Falling and Break Falling

Falling is split into two categories, falling and break falling. Falling is simply preparing your body for impact as you start towards the ground to land safely. Break falling is physically using your body and limbs to actively break into the fall. Break falling is a skill that many combat systems use to re-position the body during the impact to carry on the fight, for example if you are falling after a throw with your back turning away from your opponent the arms and legs can be used to break the fall and orientate the body back towards your opponent. Primoris shows basic falling and break falling, to ensure the student can be thrown safely during class.

Falling to the side is the most common way to fall and most of the time it is possible from different positions to orientate onto your side for the fall. In this image the impact is taken on the major muscle groups; the shoulders and thighs. Avoid landing on joints like knees and elbows. The right arm has been brought up to cover the head and the left is helping to control the fall. Notice the left leg is in the air, this is because the body should be relaxed when falling.

This fall should be repeatedly practised from both sides. ▲

This image now shows a break fall to the side. The body is still relaxed, however the right arm has been used to slap the ground the moment before the body lands to take the impact out of the landing. With practise, this slap can be used to orientate the body during the fall to a more favourable position. The head is kept tucked in, which although sounds obvious, is an important skill to practise with all falls. ▲

Falling and Break Falling

(Continued from previous page)

Falling flat backwards is something to try and avoid, you should always aim to roll onto your side. There are times however, during certain throws and falls, where it is unavoidable. In this image, both arms are used to break the fall, by slapping the ground with the palms down. It is important to try and take the impact on your arms to take pressure off the back. You should avoid any contact between your lower back and the ground. Orientate your body so that you land across the shoulder blades. Whilst this can be uncomfortable, it is preferable. Kicking out a leg can help present your shoulder blades to the floor by giving you body a more horizontal profile, the leg can also be kicked out to act as a counterweight to reduce the impact on your back and also to kick your opponent. With all falling, remember to exhale as you fall to avoid being winded. ▲

As with falling flat backwards, sometimes you can't avoid falling flat forwards. When falling forward avoid the temptation to stop the fall with straight locked out arms and taking any impact on the knees, in this image the knees are well above the ground, and the position of the arms as depicted show the impact being taken across the forearms with the hands on the ground to protect against the head hitting the floor.

What these basics show are guidelines as each person will fall differently. What is also important to bear in mind are the conditions of the throw; you may have your hands tied up so they cannot be used to break into the fall. As long as you remember to avoid, where possible, contact with the joints and the floor; your head hitting the ground and you remember to exhale, at least you will minimise the effect of being thrown or tripping. ▲

Falling Practice

Falling in the ways shown should be practised in isolation from a crouch position first, once students are comfortable with the basic idea a good exercise is to stand and simply practise falling onto a mat from different body positions and angles repeatedly. Remember, your body does not fall like a tree, you collapse in stages; legs, hips, body.

How Not to Fall

This is how not to fall

This image shows a common cause of injury when falling, since instinct normally tells the body to stop a fall by sticking out an arm or arms. This will however, mean the force of the fall is taken on the wrists and elbows, which is something to be avoided. ▲

This is how not to fall

Try to avoid using elbows to stop a fall. From a lot or grappling positions and especially throws to the side it is easy to land with an elbow first. Instead either roll the shoulder into the fall and keep the elbow high, or straighten the arm and break into the fall as depicted previously. ▲

This is how not to fall

In this image the impact has been taken on the knee, which is another common cause of injury. When falling like this, the body should be turned onto the side to take the impact onto the thighs and shoulders rather than joints. ▲

Unarmed Introduction

Fiore gives us a lot of unarmed knowledge through his Abrazare and Daga sections, but these are not complete. Within Primoris we will show you the basics of unarmed that can be built upon by the later levels, yet can still be used within an actual fight.

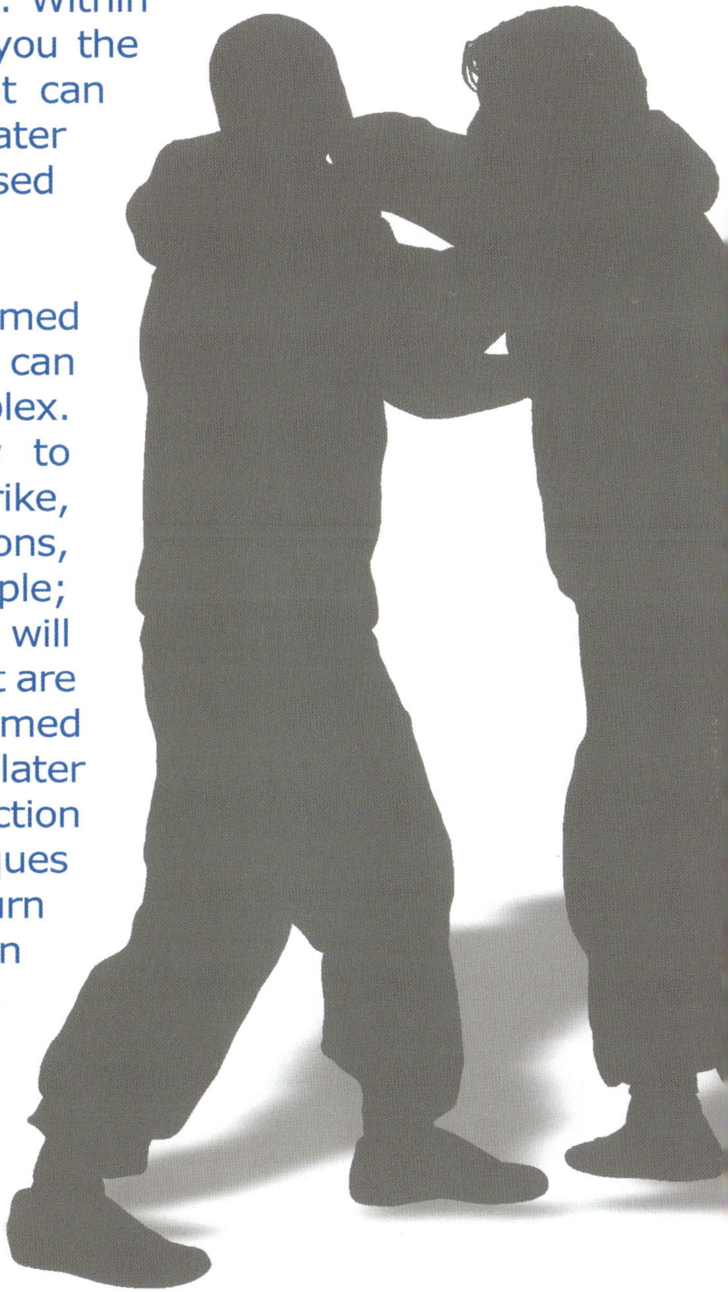

Any form of unarmed combat is difficult as it can be both fast and complex. Through learning how to strike and where to strike, with simple body positions, and then how to grapple; grip and throw you will have the basic skills that are necessary for an unarmed fight. After this, in later levels, it is the introduction of additional techniques and methods that will turn a student into an advanced, or expert, unarmed fighter.

Fiore's system has historical social constraints, but it does not mean that his principles cannot have a wider application.

Unarmed Posta

Unarmed Positions

Fiore shows four unarmed positions (Posta), and while you can effectively fight from each, they are tailored to a specific set of objectives. The Posta are fluid positions and can either be positions to wait in, to cover into, to strike from and into or to use when grappling.

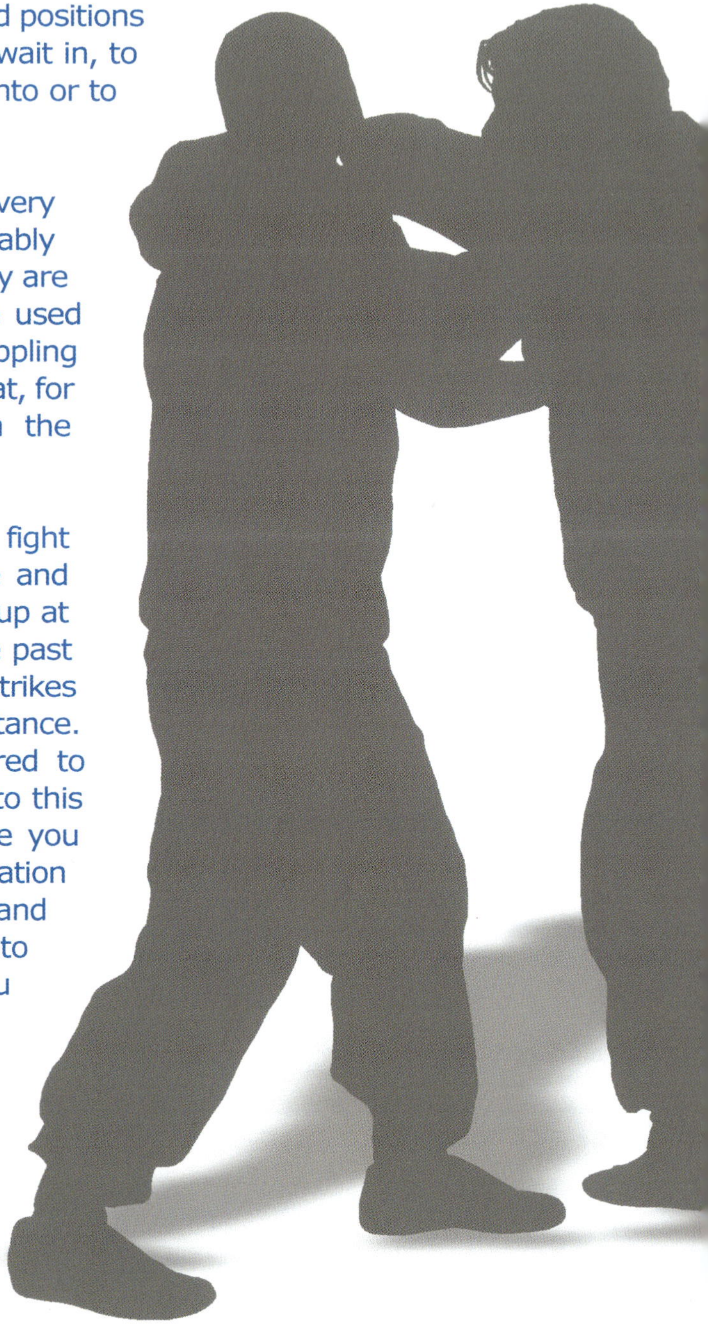

The Posta themselves can look very unorthodox and this is probably due to the context in which they are used. The Unarmed Posta are used primarily to close into grappling distance, since unarmed combat, for matters of life and death in the period, involved grappling.

It is very difficult to end a fight quickly with just strikes alone and generally most real fights end up at a close distance. Once you are past the range of effectively using strikes you are now at grappling distance. The unarmed Posta are tailored to effectively and quickly close into this distance, because that's where you want to be to end a confrontation quickly, by breaking the neck and limbs, throwing the opponent to ground etc.. Remember if you are fighting for your life, you want to deal with your opponent as quickly as possible, grappling is an effective way of seriously hurting your opponent and ending the fight quickly.

Unarmed Posta

Unarmed Positions

In Primoris only a basic understanding of the full use of the Unarmed Posta is needed, and drills are included to help with the understanding of how to use them in their basic form.

All the Unarmed Posta can be done on both sides of the body and are fluid positions, since fighting itself is fluid. You use them as a guideline to achieve an advantage, which means that there are times when you do not have to always rigidly stick to exact form with them if the situation does not warrant it.

In the next level of training, Secundus, more detail is given about tactics to use when facing your opponent in a given Posta, and which actions are best suited to which situation.

The Unarmed Posta

Posta Frontale ▲ **Porta di Ferro ▲** **Posta Longa ▲** **Dente di Zenghiar ▲**

Porta di Ferro

Iron Door

Porta di Ferro appears in the same form in the Dagger section of the system. The Posta has the arms low and held by the waist over each thigh. While from the onset it would appear that this Posta has certain risks since the upper body is left open, in practice it is a very useful and versatile position to fight from and move into.

By having the hands low you are taking the low line. You can, for example, come up to cover against a strike or grab and close in. Since the aim is always to close, Porta di Ferro allows you to keep your hands out of the way to avoid being grabbed and to react to what your opponent is giving you without committing to anything whilst in position. Naturally, you have to raise your arms to close and to avoid being hit, but with this Posta you fight from a seemingly unprepared and inoffensive position and move into different Posta or Strikes whilst keeping your opponent confused about what you are doing and where your hands are going to be. In much the same way that some modern Boxers fight with the lead hand low.

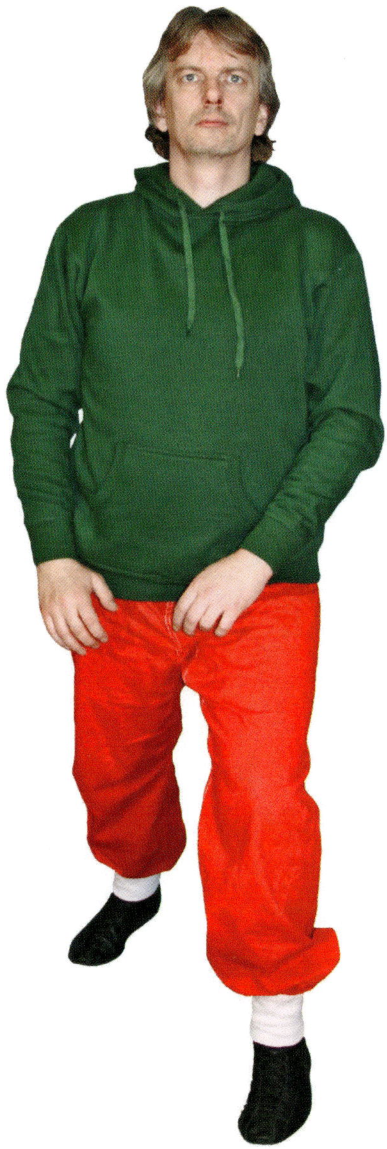

Posta Frontale

Front Position

This Posta is not too dissimilar to positions in other unarmed combat systems. It is a good platform for fist fighting, but ultimately is used for covering against strikes and closing into grappling holds. The Posta itself is also good to strike into for example a double strike to the chest or face.

The legs are bent and the weight of your body can vary, being over the front or rear leg depending on the situation. The arms are held with a bend in the elbow and at the height of your upper chest with your hands open.

Dente di Zenghiar

Boar's Tooth

This is a strange looking position at first glance and a lot about its use is in the name – Boar's Tooth. If you think of a wild Boar, they have two large teeth/tusks coming out from each side of their mouth and protruding upwards. When Boars fight they use these tusks coming forward and swinging the head up and down to cut and pierce.

Attacking with this Posta is similar to the way Boars attack, at close range straight strikes are no longer practical, but hooks, upper cuts and hammer fists (see strikes) are. Dente di Zenghiar is used for closing with these powerful strikes into grappling range and is a very good Posta to cover and defend from.

Like the other Posta the weight distribution can vary onto each foot. Most of the time however, the weight is even over both feet. The lead arm is generally always formed over the lead foot, although with covers and strikes etc, this can change.

Posta Longa

Long Position

This is Posta Longa and has several key uses. The primary use is to 'Prese' in, which means to come in behind the arm to find a hold/lock on your opponent. Posta Longa is also a position to strike into and from, keeping behind the arm and using it to probe and strike at openings your opponent presents. This Posta is not really used for standing toe to toe with multiple exchanges of strikes since it is hard to defend with only one arm forward, but is used more for a singular cover or heavy strike coming through to enter grappling range.

The position is also used for keeping an opponent at distance, by using it as what modern martial artists call 'The Fence'. The Fence is created by the fact that you have your arm out at length and this acts as a barrier your opponent must deal with to close in. The rear arm is poised for delivery of a heavy blow, to come up to cover against an attack to the offside or to find a low hold on your opponent. The high arm is formed over the lead foot and there is a slight bend to the elbow.

Unarmed Posta Drills

To help give a basic understanding of how the Posta are used there are several drills in Primoris. Please bear in mind that these drills are to help formulate an idea of usage and movement and not necessarily how to use them in an engagement.

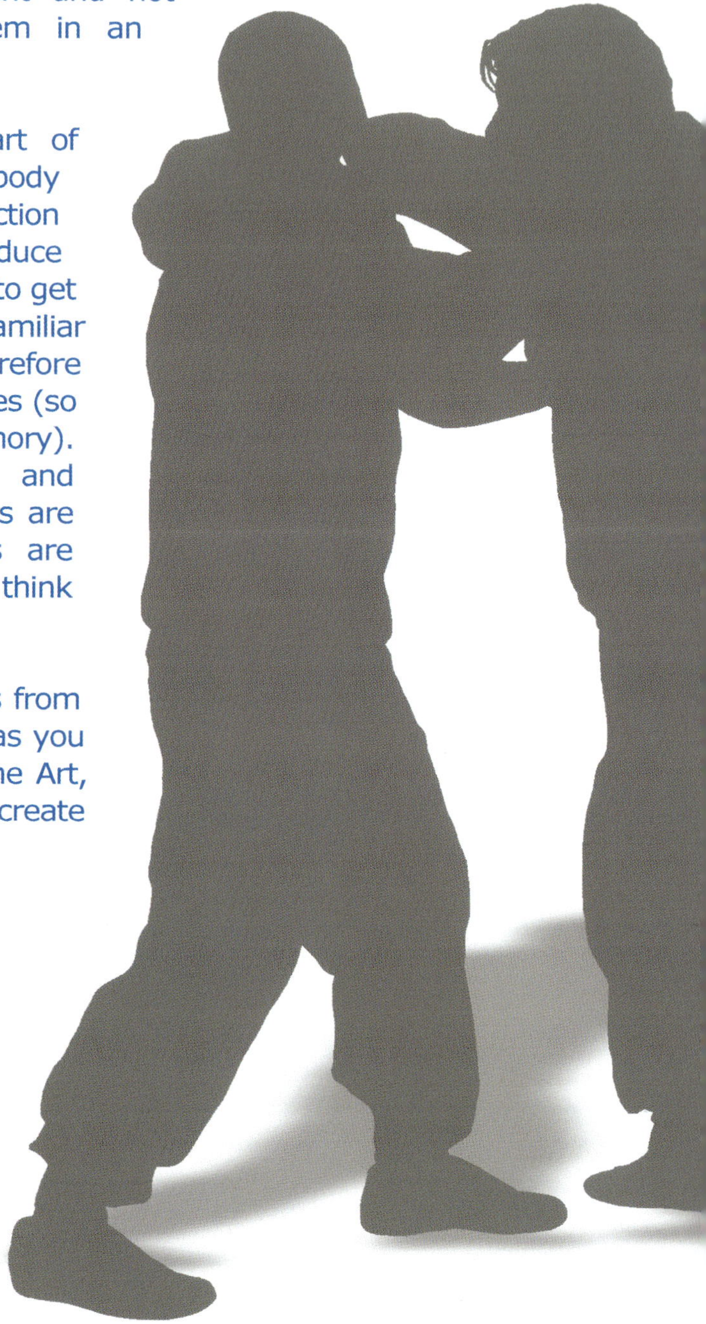

Drills form an important part of training because they get the body used to using techniques in action and can also be used to introduce an element of unpredictability to get the body used to recognising familiar positions during a fight and therefore help condition trained responses (so called muscle memory). Engagements can be fast and frenzied and trained responses are vital for times when things are happening to fast to think effectively.

The following drills are a basis from which you can work. As long as you stay within the principles of the Art, then you are encouraged to create your own drill combinations.

Unarmed Posta Drills

Basic Unarmed Posta Drill

Using the Footwork from Primoris, practise transitioning through the four unarmed Posta by changing position each time you take a step. Remember to vary the types of footwork you are using. This is a simple drill intended to get you used to taking up the Posta from different positions and is great for anyone who is not used to forming guards. When you have become more comfortable with the rest of the drills in this section and the striking come back to this drill and add those elements in so that it becomes almost like shadow boxing. This drill can also be an effective post stretch warm-up.

Posta Frontale ◄

Porta di Ferro ►

Posta Longa ◄

Dente di Zenghiar ►

Unarmed Posta Drills

Dente di Zenghiar – Inside Cover Drill

Green repeatedly steps forward using Posta Longa on each side with each step, Red uses Dente di Zenghiar to cover on the inside with each step backwards. Both are using Mezza Volta.

You can vary how deep you go with the cover for different advantages. For example, you can close right in with the Posta so that you are immediately in grappling range. You can also vary how much you come offline, to open up your opponent and zone away from their other hand. Be aware however, that this is not a block, it is a cover, so be careful not to be too aggressive with the offline movement into the high arm as you will be at risk of wide spacing yourself and pulling your opponent's other hand immediately into play.

Also practise this drill coming forward with the Dente di Zenghiar, as your opponent steps back into Posta Longa.

Unarmed Posta Drills

Posta Frontale – Inside Cover Drill

Green steps forward into Posta Longa. Red uses Posta Frontale to come up and cover against the inside of the arm. As Red is covering on the inside with this Posta ideally the same leg as Green's should be forward, so if Green has the right leg forward Red should also have the right leg forward to make the Frontale cover, being careful not to turn too much into the cover and expose the right side of the body to Green's other hand.

This Posta Frontale cover can be used to control the arm or cover against it to then close in. Once you have completed a cover step back into Porta di Ferro so you are out of distance and repeat on the other side as your partner steps in again with Posta Longa on the other side. Once you have worked backwards for 6 steps swap the person doing the cover.

You should also try this same drill but covering with a step forward rather than back as your partner steps in with Posta Longa, remembering to fall back into Porta di Ferro afterwards just to keep the drill working.

Unarmed Posta Drills

Posta Frontale - Outside Drill

Green steps forward into Posta Longa, Red uses Posta Frontale to come up and cover against the outside of the arm. As Red is now coming to the outside with an offline movement into Posta Frontale the opposite leg to Green's should be forward, so if Green's right leg is forward, Red's left leg should be forward. ▶

The simplest way to remember which leg to have forward when using Posta Frontale to Cover, is that if you are making the cover to the left of your body the right leg is forward, and on the right the left leg is forward. While this is not always possible, it is important to aim for the correct leg to be forward. ◀

Unarmed Posta Drills

Other Posta Drills

Dente de Zenghiar - Outside Cover

As with Dente di Zenghiar Inside Cover Drill, Green steps in with a Posta Longa, this time however Red uses Dente di Zenghiar to cover on the outside of the arm. Coming to the outside with Dente di Zenghiar can be difficult, but during unarmed combat the situation does arise where you can use this action to close in on the outside. ▶

Posta Frontale – Frontale against Frontale

Green Steps in to using Posta Frontale to try and take a hold of Red's head. Red uses Posta Frontale to step offline and come to the outside of Green to push at the arm to stop the head grab. Try this drill stepping both into and away from your partner and also alternating from covering the left arm and right arm. ◀

Posta Longa – Inside Line

Red and Green both take up Posta Longa, with Red taking the inside line. Green then steps forward into Posta Longa on the right and Red reacts by stepping back into Posta Longa on the left still maintaining the inside line. Repeat this six times and then swap the person stepping forward so you work in turns stepping backwards and forwards. Remember to use the Accrease foot movement before you Mezza Volta forwards or Backwards. ▶

Unarmed Posta Drills

Other Posta Drills

Posta Longa – Outside Line

As with the Posta Longa Inside Line Drill, Green steps in changing from Posta Longa on one side to the other, Red steps back into Posta Longa on the outside of the attackers arm. Repeat this six times and the change the person stepping forward.

This will require an offline movement to do correctly, Accrease the rear foot before you step backwards. As your opponent steps in you are looking to either use your own Posta Longa to simulate making contact to the head over the top of their arm, or to push at the elbow, but ultimately this drill is used to demonstrate finding an opening to close into grappling with the Posta. ►

Posta Longa – Outside Line with opposite hand.

Green steps in changing from Posta Longa on one side to the other, much the same as the Inside Line Drill Red is looking to come to the outside of Green's Posta Longa but now by using the opposite arm. So as Green steps in with the right arm, Red is also using the right arm. Again this can be to simulate a strike to the head or take control of the arm to then close into grappling range. ◄

Primoris Posta Drills Summary

The Posta Drills are in Primoris as a basis for future drills using Posta. As strikes and techniques start to be mastered these basic drills are then adapted to incorporate new elements so that they evolve. So remember the Posta drills in Primoris are to practice form and are not techniques. In total there are nine Posta Drills in Primoris:

Basic Posta Drill
Posta Longa – Inside Line
Posta Longa – Outside Line
Posta Longa – Outside Line with opposite hand
Dente di Zenghiar – Inside Cover
Dente di Zenghiar - Outside Cover
Posta Frontale – Inside cover
Posta Frontale – Outside cover
Posta Frontale – Frontale against Frontale

Unarmed Targets

Fiore tells us in his manual his key targets for abrazare are:

- **Eyes**
- **Nose**
- **Chin (which includes the neck)**
- **Flanks**

More often than not unarmed combat is about slowly reducing your opponent's ability to fight with collective injuries. These targets are noted because of how effective they are to injure in unarmed combat, but obviously all areas of an opponent should be considered a target. The idea is to injure these areas on your opponent to either end the fight or gain an advantage to apply other techniques.

Unarmed Targets

(Continued from previous page)

Eyes

The eyes are very vulnerable and can be injured in a number of ways, Fiore shows the thumbs being used to poke into the eye sockets. Attacking your opponent's eyes is a sure way to gain an advantage since the body has reflex actions which come into play whenever pressure or pain is felt in this area. It is easy to find an eye socket with a finger or to strike at the eyes from all distances in unarmed combat and in most cases the damage will be sufficient to completely disrupt an opponent's ability to fight, making the eyes a key target in unarmed and indeed armed combat.

Unarmed Targets

(Continued from previous page)

Nose

Similarly to the eyes, the body has certain reflex actions which involuntarily happen when the nose is hurt. Even a light blow will make the eyes water, disrupting vision and a bleeding nose will hamper breathing. Heavier blows and pressure to the nose will cause it to break, which is very painful. Injuring the nose may not always end an engagement but again the nose is a key target because of the effect of pain from this area on an opponent and on their ability to keep fighting effectively.

Unarmed Targets

(Continued from previous page)

Chin – Including the neck

Fiore notes the chin as being a primary target and this includes the neck. Striking the chin area and specifically the point of the chin can have a massive effect on an opponent. A good, well aimed, strike to this area can easily render them unconscious. The chin can be struck in a number of ways, with a closed fist, open hand, elbow etc.

You neck is your lifeline, your windpipe and major arteries to the brain are all vulnerable in the neck either with chokes, holds or strikes. Throughout the system the neck is a key target. With unarmed you are looking to strike at the neck or to choke your opponent by specifically targeting either the windpipe or carotid arteries. There are some basic drills in the grappling basics section of this book and further information to help give an understanding how to target the neck area.

Unarmed Targets

(Continued from previous page)

Flanks

The flanks are each side of the body from the hip to the armpit. With unarmed combat and grappling these areas are usually well presented for injury and the effect of striking and damaging these areas can be great. The main area of the flanks is the ribs and ribs are easy to injure. The floating ribs (the lower ribs) are thin bones and damaging/breaking them can be achieved with little more than a stern punch. As the flanks are often exposed in unarmed combat, strikes can often be employed to cause injury and gain an advantage for more effective techniques.

Unarmed Strikes

Fiore does not show many strikes in his system and there are many reasons why this is the case. It may be because the focus is not on striking but rather on grappling or because Fiore is showing what makes his system unique and striking can be learned from anywhere. In any case, The Exiles focus on building rounded fighters and you cannot enter into grappling without a good understanding of striking.

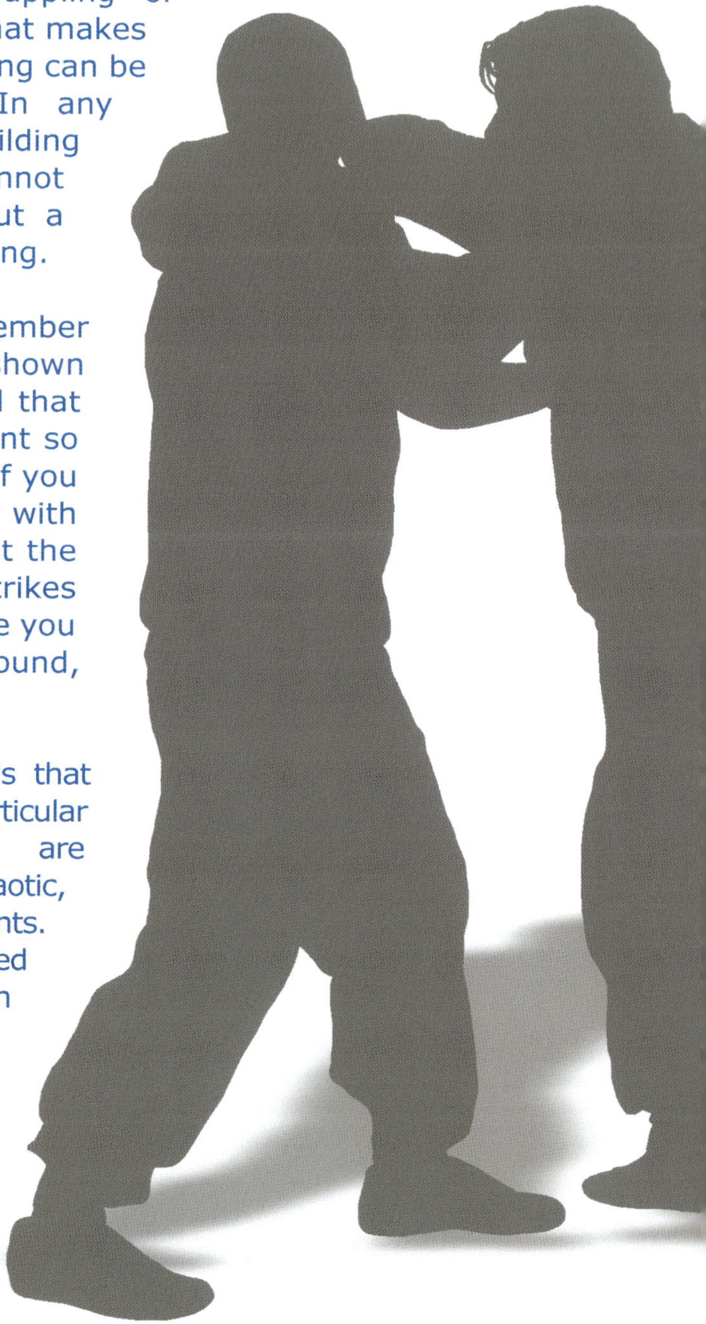

One thing is vital to remember however, all of the striking shown is focused on one thing and that is to soften up your opponent so you can close and grapple. If you finish an engagement with strikes alone then great, but the sole focus must be to use strikes to close into a position where you can break limbs, throw to ground, etc.

Another thing to remember is that with all combat, in particular unarmed combat, things are aggressive, frenzied and chaotic, even with well versed combatants. When practising unarmed combat, always try to bear in mind the context of the intention. If you are securing an arm lock on your opponent they would not stand and simply let you do it, they would fight back, so you have to make sure in practice that the technique is smooth, powerful and that you understand you will take hits and will need to have options for failure of the technique.

Unarmed Strikes

Unarmed combat is very much a case of hurting more than you are being hurt. Unless you are lucky, you should expect to take damage during a confrontation.

There are obviously lots of different ways to strike with the body and it is important not to limit your options. In combat it can be all or nothing. Within Primoris the basics are taught and in this book only the basics are covered since whole books can be written on any of the points in this section. It is vital, however to remember that you do not fight for your life with rules. If it takes burying your fingers into your opponent's eye sockets to get a throw working then you would do it. Not in training though!

In Primoris students are taught to use different body parts to strike and fists and open hands to punch. It is all about tailoring the strike to what you are doing, and utilising your body to make efficient hits. An open handed strike reduces the impact to your hand making it less likely to cause yourself injury and you can then use this open hand to bind onto your opponent. A closed fist, however, will improve the chances of, for example, rendering an opponent unconscious because the contact will be bone to bone.

Unarmed Strikes

Forearms, elbows, knees, head, feet, fingers, shoulders, etc, can all be effectively employed in given actions and times. Never underestimate the power of an open handed slap.

With striking there is a simple rule to remember:

MASS x ACCELERATION = FORCE

which means to effectively strike with good force you need either lots of mass with a strike or lots of speed. Fighters have to find a good combination of both depending on the strike, since mass with no speed will make a strike slower, but a strike with speed and not enough mass will mean the strike will be fast but will not have a great deal of force.

Different strikes require the generation of power from different parts of your body, you must remember that punching from the arms alone is never going to be as strong as using the hips and legs to help with the generation of force. Striking is an art in itself and in later levels a lot more refinement and technique is introduced. One of the hardest aspects to master with strikes is closing into grappling range behind them. In time, students learn to set up several different strikes to key targets depending on the situation as they close in.

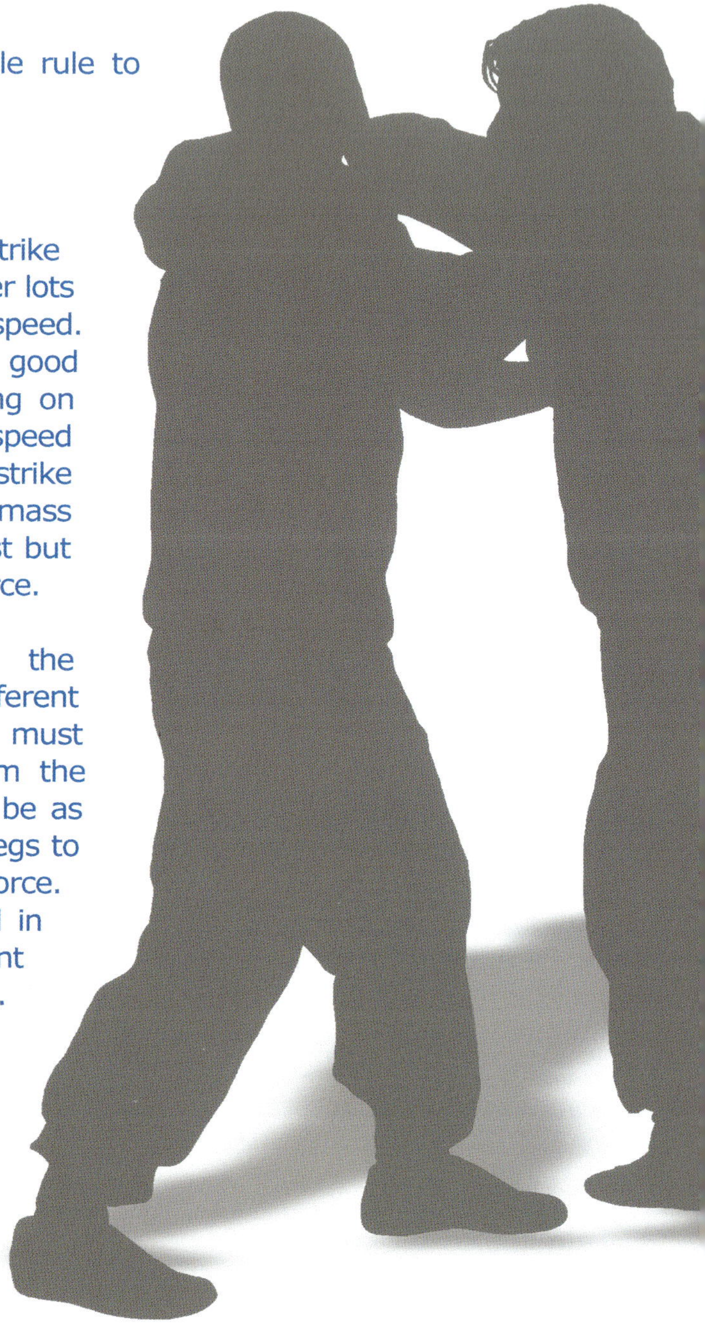

Unarmed Strikes

The Jab

A jab from Posta Longa is a straight strike from the lead hand. This can be done with an open or closed hand and with different orientations of the hand for example a vertical fist or horizontal fist. A Jab is a great strike to start to open your opponent up to either follow with a more powerful strike or to close in behind.

Since Jabbing does not involve a step it is a fast strike, but not as powerful as others. Power can be added to a jab with a sharp flick forward of the hips and a twist of the leg. Alternatively a small step with the lead foot can be used to add some mass to the strike. ►

A jab is made from Posta Longa. ▲

Unarmed Strikes

The Cross

A cross is a straight punch from the rear hand, in these images a cross is being delivered from Posta Frontale. You can see how the force is being generated from the hips and a twist of the legs. You can also step with the cross for added force, but the strike will be slower than without a step. Another tactic is to come offline with the front foot slightly, using an accrease, to deliver the strike into your opponent's centre line. ▲

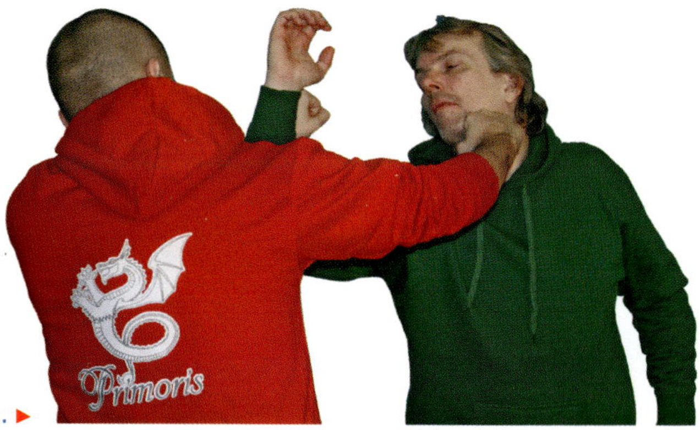

Red has launched a cross to Green's face. ▶

Unarmed Strikes

The Hook

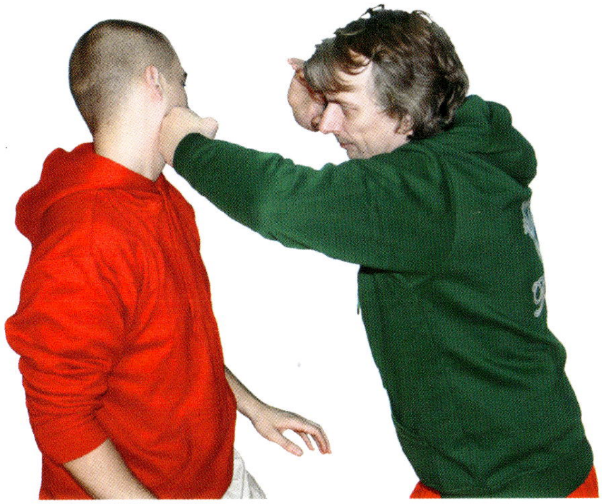

Hooks are very powerful strikes that are used at close range and are essential when grappling. They are close range strikes because they are wide spaced and at distance can be easily seen. There are lots of different ways to deliver a hook but most of these are down to preference and effect. In both these images a right hook is delivered from Posta Frontale. Power to the strike is again generated from the hips and also with the shoulder coming forward and the opposite shoulder being flicked back slightly. This image also illustrates clearly the twist of the rear leg to help with power generation and to stabilise the body.

Hooks can be done from both sides and can target the head or the body, from the lead or rear hand and both with or without a step. The orientation of the hand can make a big difference to the effect of the strike for example a vertical fist in behind the back of the jaw. With all strikes it is important to keep the wrist straight, in both images the wrist is angled in the direction of impact to the head. ▲

This is the ideal place to launch a Hook from, Red has covered against a Hook to the side of the head with a cover from Dente di Zenghiar and the distance is close enough for a counter Hook. Even if Green were to have both hands up, or even by launching his own strike, the Hook from Red's right hand would carry a lot of power and if timed right, could come in behind Green's attack or defence. ►

Unarmed Strikes

The Uppercut

The Uppercut is another important, powerful close range strike. In this image the strike would be to the jaw and the power is again generated from the body. With Uppercuts, additional power can be added to the strike by dropping your weight at the knees a few inches or so and then using your legs to twist and drive upwards to strike. The arm should be the last part of the body moving when it hits the target to get an additional kick of speed. ◂

Red has launched an Uppercut to Green's Jaw. Even if Green were to have both hands up, the Uppercut could be sent straight through the middle from here. As with all strikes, the idea would be to close in immediately to grappling range. ▸

Unarmed Strikes

The Hammer Fist

Hammer Fists are versatile strikes that use the side of the hand or forearm to strike down at your opponent. This strike is often used when grappling to target your opponent's face or collar bone, and if when grappling your opponent bends down and exposes the back of their head this is a great strike to use. Hammer Fists can be used after a successful of even unsuccessful Uppercut since the hand is already high. ◄

Here Green has used the Hammer Fist to strike down onto Red's collar bone. ►

Unarmed Strikes

The Elbow and the Head

Elbows are often employed as close range strikes. Striking with the elbow is done much the same way as with a hook and because of the greater density of bone in the elbow can delivery a very hard strike. In later levels the use of elbows is widened and they are also used for coming vertically into the face or striking lower into the ribs. Essentially everything you can punch at you can hit with an elbow.

The head can be used a great deal in unarmed combat and even in weapon play. Often the hands can be wide spaced or bound and the head can be used to strike at the opponent with devastating effect. When striking with the head, the chin is kept low (as is should always be during unarmed combat to protect the chin) and the very top of the forehead is used to make contact. The neck is kept straight and the power is delivered from the body to reduce exposing the face and to minimise the risk of damaging the neck.

Unarmed Strikes

The Knee and Biting

Since the legs have the most powerful muscles, striking with a knee can be a very effective strike to use in grappling. Care must be taken not to come off balance and it is always advisable to have a firm hold of your opponent so that you have more support when you deliver the strike. By pulling your opponent down as your knee is coming up you can also add power to the strike.

Biting in the modern arena would be considered a dirty tactic, however when fighting for your life biting should always be open to consideration if the opportunity arises. Key areas to focus on with bites are the nose, ears and neck, however any area open can be bitten. What must be remembered with bites is the risk of infection, however if fighting for survival that may be a small concern.

Unarmed Striking Drills

To help gain an understanding of effectively striking and defending there are a few simple drills in Primoris.
The idea of these drills is to enhance them over time with new skills so that ultimately they end up like a structured sparring session, where different elements can be focused on, but all skills are there to be used when appropriate and at the discretion of the fighter based on given situations.

The idea with all the drills should be to start slowly to get the mind used to trained responses. The following drills provide the basis and it is up to the individual to use them as a basis to build their own style.

Unarmed Striking Drills

"Patsy" Drill

The first drill is called Patsy, and can be used by students as soon as the basics of striking and covering are practised. The aim is to practise covering against incoming strikes and gaining an opening to either close (the ultimate aim of Abrazare) or counter strike. The drill is called Patsy because you are taking advantage of your opponent's strikes to create your own threat. The drill itself has lots of different elements happening but basically your opponent is striking at you and you are simply using movement, in Posta, with open handed covers and slaps at the strikes to redirect them and gain an advantage.

A few important points with this drill; the drill uses covers not blocks to defend (there are no blocks as such in the entire curriculum), in unarmed terms a block is a wide spaced action and is physically powered into strikes to stop them (mass vs. mass), a cover is used to shield against incoming strikes rather than actively working against them. In frenzied unarmed combat, it is difficult if not impossible to use blocks to actively defend against a flurry of strikes. With this drill slaps are also used against the incoming strikes to redirect the force. While a slap may sound like a ridiculous way to defend against an incoming strike, they are employed at distance and against straight strikes, as the range closes down, covers are then used.

Before you start with this drill, there are a few small exercises to help understand the idea of how slaps work to defend against straight strikes at distance.

Exercise One. With a partner stand at a distance where, with an outstretched arm, they can just touch your chest. In a stance with either foot forward have your hands down by your sides. The challenge is for your partner to touch your chest as fast as they can with their hand. Your aim is to bring a hand up to redirect or slap their striking hand away. You can only use one hand at a time and the other hand must remain by your side, each time you have slapped your opponent's hand away return your hand to your side.

Unarmed Striking Drills

(Continued from previous page)

When redirecting and slapping you have the choice of slapping your partner's hands down or to each side to defend and create openings, both you and your partner can use either hand at any time. After a few minutes, start to bring in footwork and slipping offline as well as going both backwards and forwards into the strike.

Exercise Two. The same as the first exercise, but now have your hands on your head, whilst using the same principles.

Using the four unarmed Posta, with your partner now striking using straight strikes (Jabs and Crosses), use slaps and movement to redirect and avoid the strikes. When you gain an opening, try to reply with your own strike to your partner as fast as you can, your partner now also has the option of defending and returning with their own strikes so you are both working together. Remember this drill is at the very edge of striking distance and foot movement is the key. Try to experiment as much as possible with different angles and responses, the great thing about this kind of drill is that the more you do it, the more you learn what is effective and what is not with no real additional instruction.

As a variation, give the drill some structure. Have the attacker throw in two strikes from the right followed by two from the left, as the defender. The aim is to use covers and slaps followed by counter strikes to the head and body after each strike. You are looking to move to the outside of the first strike and counter strike, then to the inside of the second strike to counter strike, followed by the same with the attackers strikes from the left. So you are moving to the outside, then the inside, then outside and inside of the four incoming strikes and counter striking. This may take a few attempts to get correct, but can really help to improve striking skills.

Unarmed Striking Drills

Cover Drill

While the Patsy drill is great for practising the defence of strikes at the edge of striking distance, when stronger strikes are coming in from different angles (for example hooks) and at closer distance more solid defences are needed. There are four covers to use in this drill, inside and outside covers, although the covers in this drill are best used for straight strikes.

Red has made an inside cover against Green's strike (a jab) this could just as easily be done on Red's left side against a right cross from green. With a partner, practise this cover on both sides and when you are comfortable start to add in your own strikes against random attacks from both sides. With this image the off hands of both people are low, this is for clarity, this cover can be done with both hands high. ◄

This image shows Red covering against a deep strike from Green on the outside. Outside covers are normally done when you have your opposite foot forward to your opponent. With a partner, practise this cover in isolation on both sides, when you have become comfortable add the two together and then at random. ►

The Drill

With the inside and outside covers shown, you can now drill the four together by having a partner throw strikes in at random, your aim is to make an appropriate defence against the strikes. Remember, these are not blocks, but are fluid defences where you are always moving and using only enough power to defend against the strikes. Once you have become comfortable with these covers in the drill, add in your own strikes in response so that both you and your partner are working with this drill in turn very much like a structured spar.

Unarmed Striking Drills

Deep Cover Drill

Deep covers are employed when a strike is made at very close distance, and like all covers the idea is to protect vulnerable areas. From this image, you can see that Green has made a right hook to Red's head (keeping the left arm low for clarity of image). Due to the distance involved, Red has responded with a high cover using the left arm. This is a deep cover, and can be done on both sides, Red's options here are to counter strike and re-gain distance, or close in.

Deep covers can also be used against low strikes to the body, In this image Green has made a right hook to Red's flank. Red has dropped the arm with the elbow tucked in to protect the ribs and flank using the arm.

Practise these deep covers against hooks to both sides of the head, once you are comfortable, practise them at random and then combine with drills already shown in this section.

All of the techniques and drills shown in this section should be practised and then combined to effectively cover both straight strikes at distance and closer stronger angled strikes. By combining the elements in this section you effectively have, at a basic level, defences against all strikes and for Primoris this is all that is required for a framework that can be built upon. While there may not appear to be much covered with the drills in this section, there is a lot going on, and they can be taken as far as you want to get the most out of them. The secret with all combat is to have a strong basic foundation so that in the heat of confrontation, responses are quick, well practised and effective.

Throws

Throws are an important skill to learn and best employed in the middle distance range of unarmed combat. Fiore's system is focused primarily on grappling to injure your opponent before putting them to ground and throws are prevalent throughout the system.

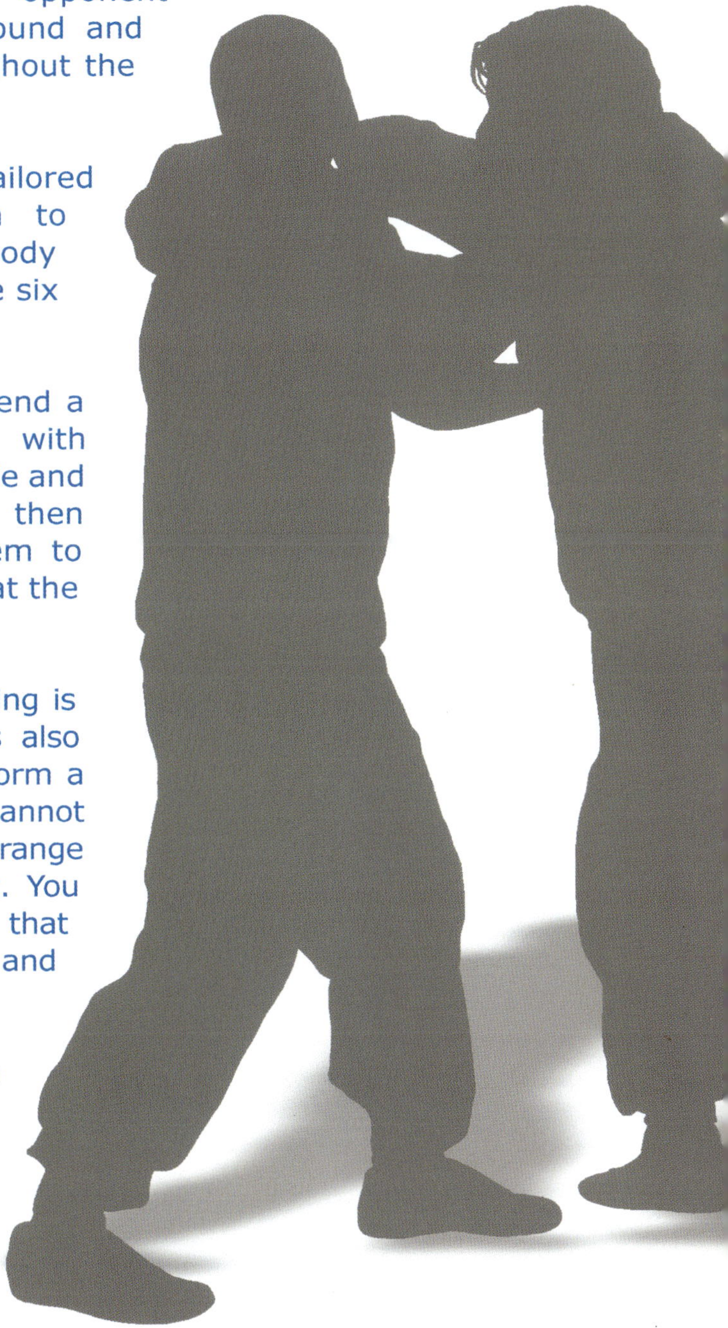

The throws in Primoris are tailored to help a student begin to understand how important body mechanics are and there are six throws in the level.

A throw in itself will rarely end a confrontation. The idea with unarmed combat is to grapple and injure your opponent and then employ a throw to put them to ground. Ideally, doing both at the same time.

Unarmed combat and grappling is naturally chaotic and this is also true when moving in to perform a throw. Remember that you cannot just step into throwing range without the risk of being hit. You have to fight your way into that range using posta, covers and counter strikes.

The six throws shown within in Primoris are:

- **The Thigh Throw**
- **The Arm Bar Throw**
- **The Cross Buttock**
- **The Neck Throw**
- **The Sacrifice Throw – used for confidence building.**
- **The Simple Leg Sweep**

The Thigh Throw

A Thigh Throw is probably the most common throw used within Martial Arts. Fiore shows a Thigh Throw and calls it a Gamberola, meaning a sort of gamble. In essence Fiore is right, the throw can be a gamble as both fighters are in the same position to throw each other.

The throw is executed by doing the following

As Green has his right leg forward, Red needs to step in with his right leg. ▼

Red will perform the throw

Red places his leg behind Green's leg with the back of his knee making contact with the back of Green's knee. Red keeps a bend in his leg and the heel of his foot off the ground once it has been placed. ▲

As Red stepped in he took hold of Green's upper body. This can be in what ever way feels comfortable, but is usually with an arm across the body and taking control of their forward arm from the inside. ▲

The Thigh Throw

(Continued from previous page)

Red performs a Tutta Volta turn whilst straightening his lead leg and placing his heel on the floor to disrupt Green's balance. Red is pulling Green over his straightening leg as he turns. ▼

Red is aiming to land Green onto his back, by Red's feet, so that it is easier to control the fight from there. ▼

This throw should be practised from both sides in isolation. After some familiarity try the following two exercises to fully understand the throw. Remember that whichever leg your opponent has forward, it is the same leg that you step forward with to throw them, so right to right and left to left.

Isolated throw drills

- With a partner, take a hold of each other's shoulders or upper body. Designate one of you to be performing the Thigh Throw. The non-thrower's task is to move around and take steps while the thrower tries to step in and execute the throw.
- With a partner, both take up a posta, designate one of you to be performing the throw and the other to be the striker. The striker should be sending in controlled blows, slower at first. The thrower is aiming to cover the strikes, step in and action the throw.

This same process should be done to help practise all throws in Primoris.

The Arm Bar Throw

The Arm Bar is a throw shown by Fiore in the dagger section and can be executed from a number of positions.

The throw works by stepping to the outside of your opponent and using your lead leg behind theirs as well as pressure on their upper body to generate the throw. Whereas with many throws you are using the same leg to step in with that your opponent has forward at the time, an Arm Bar uses the opposite leg. So if your opponent has their left leg forward, you are using your right leg to throw them.

The throw is executed in the following stages

Red will perform the throw

Green has his right leg forward so Red must step in with his left leg to the outside of Green. This will place Red's leg behind Green's lead leg with the front of his knee making contact with the back of Green's knee. ▲

The Arm Bar Throw

(Continued from previous page)

As Red steps in, his lead arm is placed across the front of Green's body. This can be over the top of Green's arm or underneath as long as Red is barring Green's body with his lead arm. Red uses his rear arm to take hold of Green's arm for more control. ▼

Red's body is close up against Green's and is facing in the same direction. Red is both offline and beside Green. ▲

The Arm Bar Throw

(Continued from previous page)

Red completes the throw by using his arm to push Green's body over his leg as he turns. Red causes Green to land by his feet so that he has complete control of the throw. ▼

The Arm Bar Throw

(Continued from previous page)

An added element of this throw can be to use your rear arm to grab your opponent's leg as you step and it starts to come off the floor. By lifting this leg as you turn more power can be added, but in most cases control of the throw will not be as good. ▼

Always practise throws on both sides of the body

The Arm Bar and Thigh Throw should be your primary middle range throws. The legs which both you and your opponent are leading with at the start will help to dictate which throw you use. Both throws can be drilled at once by using a partner, taking hold of each other's body and having them step and move around. Look to perform the appropriate throw based on which leg they have forward at a given time. After some practice, release the hold on each other and instead cover against strikes, counter striking where necessary and stepping in to perform a throw. This is an expanded version of the throw isolation drills mentioned after the Thigh Throw itself.

The Cross Buttock Throw

A Cross Buttock is another throw which appears in many Martial Arts and is very similar in set-up to a Thigh throw with the main difference being that your opponent is thrown using your buttock.

Practise building up the throw in the following stages

In the same way as with a Thigh Throw you need to match legs. Green had his right foot forward and so Red has stepped in behind Green with his right leg. ▼

Red will perform the throw

Red bends his knees and keeps his back straight. He places his buttock beneath Green whilst taking hold of his body at the same time. ▲

The Cross Buttock Throw

(Continued from previous page)

With a turn, Red lifts Green by straightening his legs. Green is lifted from the ground supported on Red's buttock. ▼

For Health and Safety within training you must ensure that you control the throw and do not allow anyone to land on their neck or injure their body

Red completes the throw by rolling Green across his buttock. In a real throw Red would aim to land Green upon his upper back and head. ▲

The Cross Buttock Throw

(Continued from previous page)

With practise this can be a very effective throw and can really cause injury to your opponent. At times it can be hard to lift your opponent from the ground, especially if they have a weight advantage. Remember that when sparring or fighting, your opponent will not be so aware of what is going on and can be distracted with strikes, etc.

If a Cross Buttock Throw fails, it is easy to fall back slightly and apply a Thigh Throw as an alternative.

The Neck Throw

The Neck Throw is in Primoris to help students understand a very important principle. That is, where the head goes the body will follow. The neck throw can be dangerous to practise at speed so always take care.

The throw works by disrupting your opponent's balance using their head with a pull and twist of their body as you step back. This throw is not directly in the system but there are techniques shown where control of the head is used to injure an opponent and put them to ground. This throw is a good way to learn the basis of manipulating the head to disrupt balance.

Red will perform the throw

With either foot forward, Red takes a hold of Green by grabbing with both hands around Green's neck. This is just below the ears with both hands gripped behind Green's head. ▲

The Neck Throw

(Continued from previous page)

The foot that Red has at the rear is the direction that Green will be thrown. If Red's left foot is back then Green will be thrown to Red's left. ▼

Red pulls Green's head strongly backwards and down with a Volta Stabile twist of his body towards Red's rear foot. ▲

The Neck Throw

(Continued from previous page)

As Green loses balance and his head reaches about waist height, Red lets go of Green's neck. In realty, you would keep hold of the neck and this would cause injury or allow you to control the fight from there. Your opponent should fall behind you as you pull them downwards. ►

If your opponent is able to resist to a point where this throw cannot be done, a good alternative is to pull their head down and knee them in the face.◄

Here Green has switched from a Neck Throw to a K ee to the face of Red

This throw should only be practised in isolation, and not drilled. Should you wish to practise it at speed however or as part of a drill or with sparring, get the throw started enough to get the other person off balance and then release and reset.

The Sacrifice Throw

The Sacrifice Throw is used purely to build a student's confidence. Often people starting in Martial Arts have little experience of what it is like to be thrown or to have a person take full control of their body and place them in a position they are really not used to.

The Sacrifice Throw must be performed carefully on adequate mats, such as a heavy duty crash mat. The most important thing with this throw is to always ensure the person being thrown keeps their chin tucked in to avoid injury to the neck.

The throw is executed in the following way

Green takes a high grip on Red with both hands. ▼

Green will perform the throw

The Sacrifice Throw

(Continued from previous page)

Green pulls Red towards him as if he was sitting down. As Green does this he places his foot (either foot) into the middle of Red's pelvis and keeps his leg bent. ▼

It is this moving backwards that gives the throw its name and is why it is used as a confidence building throw.

The Sacrifice Throw

(Continued from previous page)

As Green lands on his back he straightens out his leg to throw Red over his head.▼

If the throw does not go correctly at this stage - for example, the thrower has not managed to plant their leg correctly - then you should abandon the throw. There is the very real danger that the person being thrown may land off to one side of the crash mat rather than going over the top to land safely.

The Sacrifice Throw

(Continued from previous page)

Green releases his grip as Red goes over his head. If Green has built up enough momentum Red will go straight over and will be momentarily upside down before he lands. For Red this is basically a forward roll in mid air. ▼

It can take a few attempts to get the timing of the landing and the straightening of the leg correct. Always remember to make sure the person being thrown has their chin tucked in to avoid injury when landing.

Remember this throw is for confidence building only but does help to give an appreciation of body mechanics.

The Leg Sweep

There are various forms of the Leg Sweep. Here we show a simple face-on version, which is a leg hook, that can be very handy when grappling. It does, however, mean that you can be caught off balance whilst performing this throw. So you need to bear this in mind.

The throw is executed by doing the following

Red will perform the throw

If Green has his left leg forward then Red will start with his left leg forward. If Green has his right leg forward then Red will start with his right leg forward. Red anchors himself onto Green's neck. ▲

The Leg Sweep

(Continued from previous page)

Red steps forward around the outside of Green's leading leg, using his upper body movement to disrupt Green's balance. ▼

Red quickly hook-sweeps Green's leading leg out of the way. ▲

The Leg Sweep

(Continued from previous page)

Red completes the move by pushing Green backwards and away. Green will fall as his balance has been completely disrupted.▼

Isolated throw drills

With a partner, grapple onto them. Move their weight backwards to allow for the step in and then perform the sweep. Practise this from both sides, with a different leg leading. As the technique improves, get the partner to apply more resistance to the person performing the throw.

Grappling

Grappling is the primary method shown by Fiore in unarmed combat and in many ways is the basis of the system. As previously explained the unarmed Posta are positions which are tailored to enter into the close grapple and so the grappling techniques in the system follow on from the Posta. It is vital to bear in mind the unarmed Posta at all times as by using them and their motions, during grappling, will often help make a motion or technique more effective. For example, one of the unarmed plays (techniques) shows putting an opponent to ground by essentially taking a hold of their waist around their back and performing a Posta Longa movement to their face.

Grappling is the most effective way to control an opponent and end their fight. It is much more reliable than striking and, when aggression is high, striking range most often breaks down into grappling range. Where grappling range starts can vary but a rule of thumb can be the point where the fighter with the longest arms can take a hold of an opponent's head and anywhere inwards from this point.

Grappling encompasses many different aspects but basically is the use of techniques, holds, locks, chokes and counters in order to gain a physical advantage or to escape a position. As discussed in the striking section, Fiore does not directly

Grappling

show striking in unarmed, however remember that any aspect of grappling will feature strikes and blows, because your opponent will do whatever they can to win - as you indeed should. With grappling you have to accept that you may take strikes, but by looking to gain an arm lock, for example, the aim is to give more damage than you take. Another important thing to note is that there is no ground fighting shown in the system. The idea is to grapple upright and put your opponent to ground using techniques and throws so that they cannot get back up or take you down with them. That said, the unarmed techniques in the system can be applied to the ground with slight modification, but ideally you always want to stay upright.

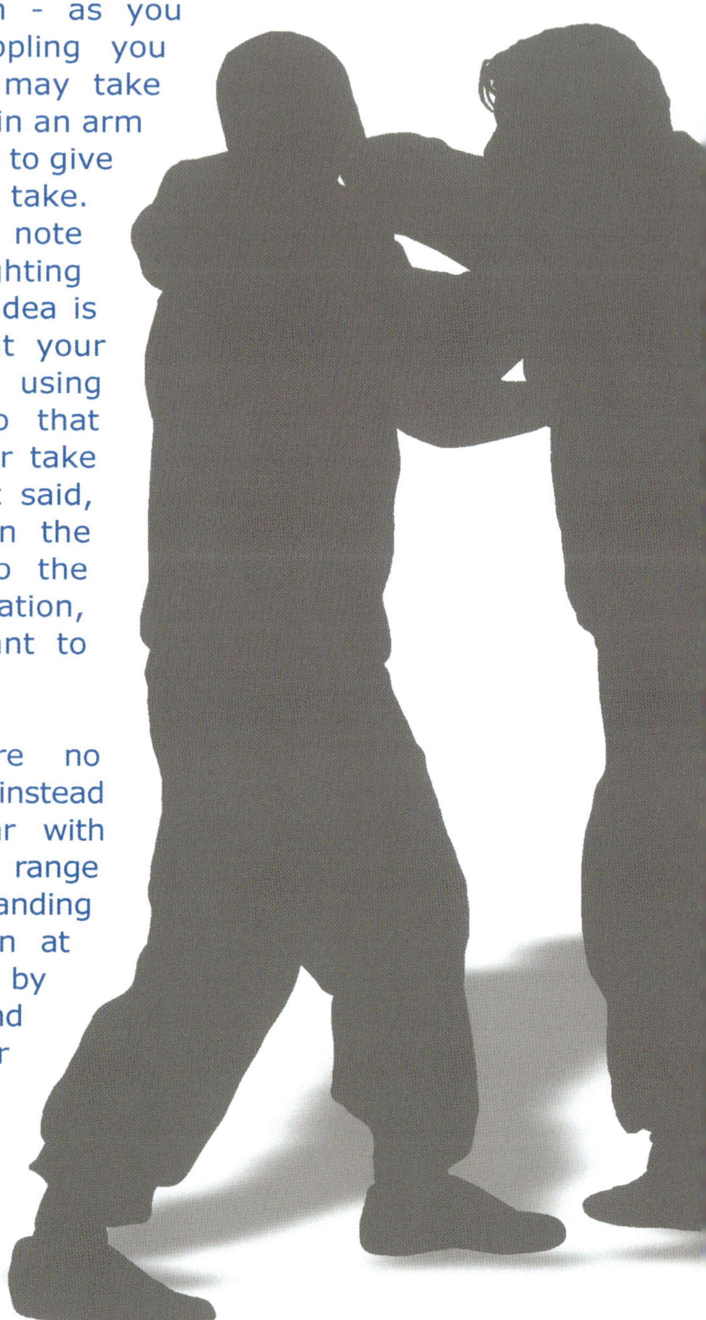

Within Primoris there are no grappling techniques taught, instead students are made familiar with firstly closing into grappling range (see striking) and understanding basic body mechanics when at grappling range - at first by using the Primoris throws and then by using holds. Together this is enough for the Primoris student to start grappling.

Grappling Holds

After some practice of moving from striking to the close and throwing, the student should already be building the basics of grappling. Together with the throws an understanding of how an opponent's body can be manipulated is being learned. The next phase is to practise some holds.

In Primoris the holds are against the head and body, since arm holds and locks are introduced from the unarmed plays and dagger in the next level - Secundus.

To help with grappling holds, there are different ways to grip your hands together when holding your opponent; some for strength; some for a quick release. Which you use vary depending on your actions and preference but the common ones are shown here.

Do Not Hold Like This

It is vitally important that you do not inter-lock your fingers. Although this may seem to be very natural it means that the knuckles can be locked onto each between your hands. If this happens and a lot of pressure is applied against your hold then you can dislocate your fingers!

Grappling Holds

Wrist Clinch

Wrist Clinch – where your left hand holds your right wrist and visa versa. This is a strong grip and good for a quick release, for example, after a throw has been started.

Red's arms are in line so he can perform a full wrist clinch. ◂

Red's arms are not in line, but at an angle to each other, so he can only perform the clinch onto one wrist. ▸

Grappling Holds

Palm Grip

Palm Grip – this grip is with both palms together with the hands turned so that you can close your fingers over your own hands. This grip is good for lifting and throwing.

As Red's arms are in a straight line he has adjusted the angle of his palm grip to give the best hold. ◄

Red is in the best position for a palm grip and can quickly pull Green down and release his grip when necessary. ►

Grappling Holds

Finger Grip

Finger Grip – This grip is easy to do and good for bigger opponents or holds across an opponent's body. Not to be confused with interlocking the fingers, which is difficult to release and can cause injury.

Red has a very strong grip across Green's lower back, which he can use to apply pressure and cause injuries to Green's back.

Red also has a strong grip when applied across Green's body, from which he can release himself quickly if required.

Grappling Holds Practice

Grappling Holds Practice One

The first stage of practice is to use a partner to apply holds whilst they are static and standing in a posta. Use the different grips from all angles around their body including from behind.

- Left hand around the head or neck and right hand around the waist
- Right hand around the head or neck and left hand around the waist
- Left hand over the shoulder linking with the right hand around the flank under the arm
- Right hand over the shoulder linking with the left hand around the flank under the arm
- Both hands around the head or neck
- Both hands around the waist

Have the passive partner change position and then repeat. Aim to move between different holds without moving away as you reset, so that you flow around their body from hold to hold.

Grappling Holds Practice Two

Have your partner move around as you apply the same holds. Build this up and add in some resistance with your partner trying to prevent the holds and moving out of them using their arms.

Grappling Holds Practice Three

Starting from striking distance have your partner throw strikes. Move into cover against these strikes and step either to the inside or outside. Now take hold of your partner, which they resist.

Build this drill up by performing throws from the holds. The most important thing is that you are effectively learning to control your opponent's body after closing.

Remember this is practice, so while you are holding it is understandable to feel vulnerable to strikes and throws from your partner.

Introduction to Dagger (Daga)

Fiore dei Liberi called this "the deadly dagger" for very good reason. Any form of short-weapon fighting is both dangerous and fast and the dagger is no different to this. It is no wonder that Fiore dedicated a large part of his system towards countering the dagger attack.

When studying the dagger you should remember that Fiore grouped the dagger with the Unarmed (Abrazare) and that a lot of unarmed techniques can also be applied at this distance – especially once the threat of the dagger has been countered.

As you study this Dagger section, remember that Fiore's system is just one integrated system and that the different weapon forms just introduce variations of application.

Within this Dagger Section you will be shown the basic fighting positions (postas); the lines of attack for the Dagger; introduced to the weapon itself and some fundamentals; given the basics of the nine Master Remedies of Dagger to counter a dagger attack and finally some drills to allow you to practise all that you have learned.

Dagger Fundamentals

As with any system or weapon form, it is important that you understand the fundamentals involved with the dagger.

For Primoris we will describe three Dagger fundamentals – the dagger itself; the dagger postas and the lines of attack. Earlier sections describe other fundamentals of equal importance – such as footwork and turning; throws and falling.

Within Primoris we will give you the grounding that you require to fully understand and apply the entire Martial Art of Fiore dei Liberi, It is, therefore, important that you fully understand the dagger used within the context of the Fiore system and, hence, how it can be applied within combat. Using the correct lines of attack, fighting positions, footwork, etc. will equip you for the techniques within the dagger section and allow you to move onto more advanced topics in later levels.

The Dagger

The Dagger used in Fiore's system is called a Rondel Dagger. This is a typical martial dagger used in the medieval and early renaissance periods. It would be worn on the right hip, for a right-handed fighter, and hence was more often drawn ready for a downward stab. The dagger itself was more commonly designed as a stabbing dagger, rather than a cutting knife.

The word Rondel means circular or round and the dagger received this name as both the Pommel and the Hand Guard were circular, or similar - e.g. octagonal. The lack of a cross guard means that the Rondel Dagger offers less hand protection, but can be moved and turned within close quarters without the risk of getting a cross-guard caught or snagged. This makes the Dagger an excellent attacking weapon.

The Blade was typically about 30cm long and as a rough guide could reach down the forearm to the elbow, giving the option of additional protection against longer edged weapons. As a stabbing weapon the blade was often triangular, although edged versions also existed, and could be used to enter small openings - such as the links in chain-mail or the gaps within armour.

The Handle was designed so that the hand would sit nicely between the two rondels of the Pommel and the Hand Guard.

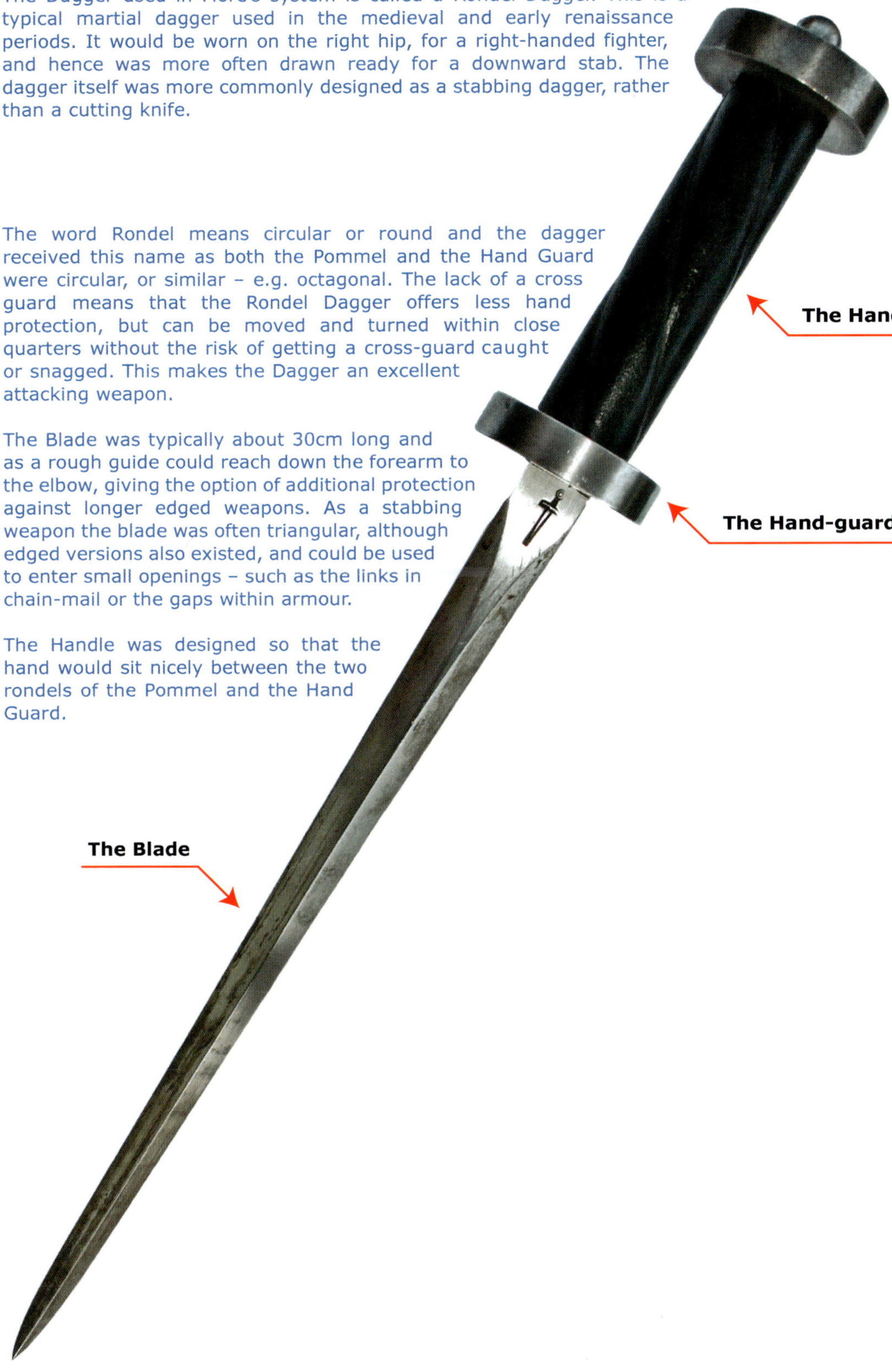

Tutta Porta di Ferro Sempia

Full Iron Door Single

Full Iron Door Single

This is the same version of Porta di Ferro that is found in the unarmed Abrazare section. Porta di Ferro is one of the most effective positional Postas and is found throughout the system.

This is Full Iron Door Single and the first of five variations that are used with dagger. It is called Full because the chest and hands are facing full-on to the opponent. It is Single as the arms are not linked or connected. ▲

Tutta Porta di Ferro Dopia

Full Iron Door Doubled

Full Iron Door Doubled

This variation of Porta di Ferro is Full because the chest and arms are straight-on to the opposing Player. It is Doubled because the hands are joined by the right hand gripping the left wrist.

This variation can form a very strong defence by covering an incoming dagger strike with both the arms. It does, however, not give as much distance between you and the incoming dagger attack as Tutta Porta di Ferro Sempia. As such it is better that you come off-line and have protection for the body and head. ▲

Mezza Porta di Ferro Dopia Incrosada

Middle Iron Door Doubled and Crossed

Middle Iron Door Doubled and Crossed

Here the dagger is held with the arms both Doubled, joined by the dagger, and Crossed and it is to the side of the body, hence it is Middle.

This is the most common position to hold a dagger for attacking and defence. From this Posta a stabbing attack can be quickly made. It is not as good for defence, though, when kept Doubled as it is a short cover and any block that isn't off-line will bring the incoming dagger very close. For this reason it is better to be wearing protection when staying Doubled and Crossed whilst being defensive with this Posta. ▲

Mezza Porta di Ferro Dopia

Middle Iron Door Doubled

Middle Iron Door Doubled

The dagger is held forward in a thrusting grip. It is to the side of the body and so it is Middle and both hands are used so it is Doubled.

This is the best position for thrusting at an opponent. It also offers the strongest defence of all the Porta di Ferro dagger Postas as it is very strong due to being Doubled and gives the best extension of reach for stopping an incoming dagger strike, regardless of whether the strike is high or low. ▲

Tutta Porta di Ferro Dopia Incrosada

Full Iron Door Doubled and Crossed

Full Iron Door Doubled and Crossed

The arms are Crossed and, with the chest and body, are straight-on to the opposing Player, so it is Full. The arms are touching, for strength, and so are Doubled.

This is a strong defensive position if wearing protection. Without protection a long cover cannot be made and the income dagger will be too close if on-line. It does, however, offer a large number of counter attack options once a good cover is made. ▲

Dagger Lines of Attack

These are the lines of attack that can be used with a Dagger

This is the most common and most natural attack. It is a downward strike from the right hand side usually into the opponent's neck. The strike can be made anywhere from the side of the head to the upper torso, but note that the lower the strike the more horizontal the angle of the attack will be. ►

This is a downward centre line strike into the opponent's face, although it can also come down into the neck and torso. The lower the strike, though, the more open the attacker is for a counter attack. ◄

Dagger Lines of Attack

(Continued from previous page)

This is a left side downward strike. It is most common to the neck, although is can be used against anywhere down from the side of the head to the upper torso. The lower the strike the more horizontal the angle of the attack will be. ►

This is the thrusting dagger strike and is normally directed just under the chest, although its angle can be towards the head and so the attack can come higher. ◄

Dagger Master Remedies

There a numerous ways to counter (remedy) a dagger attack and so Fiore grouped them into nine different Remedy Masters. In reality each Remedy Master contains several actual techniques, but within Primoris we concentrate on the basic principles of the main techniques and we will expand upon these within the next level - Secundus.

The different Master Remedies counter attacks from high and low; from the left and the right; with and without a dagger. For Primoris we have dictated a good starting position for each Remedy, but this can be changed as your training progresses.

Although we are still at a basic level of training there are some complex moves included within these Master Remedies, as it is sometimes better to learn a more difficult application and then simplify it later. An example of this is that all the high attacks are made from the attacker's right - which means that some of the Remedies will require you to adjust your footwork first. This gives you more footwork practice, but also increases your options. In later levels you will be shown that using some of these Remedies, such as Third Master, is very easy when the attack is from your opponent's left.

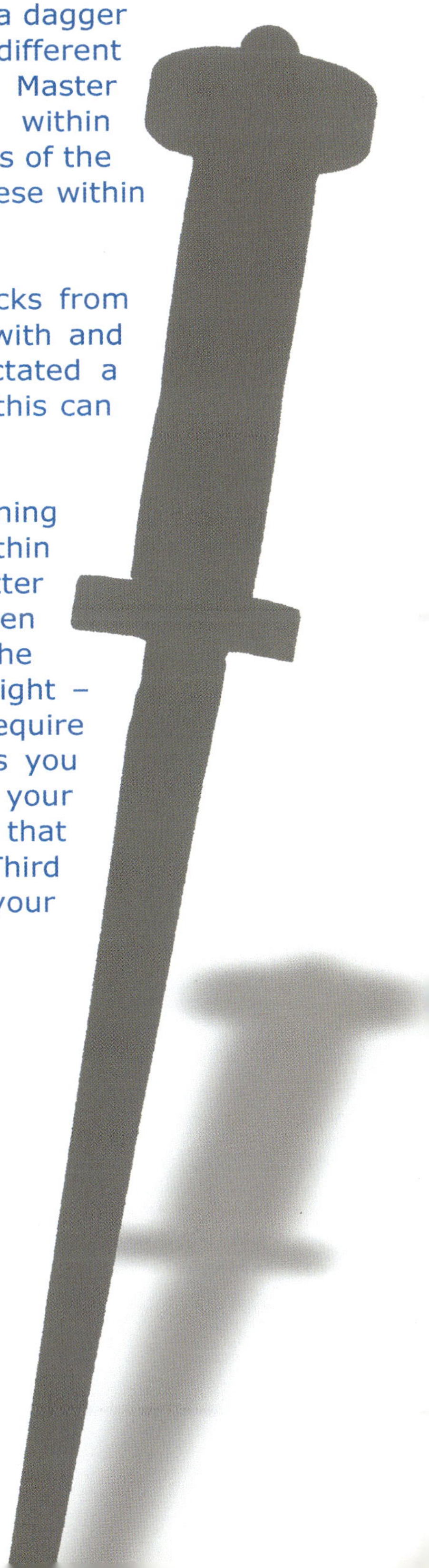

Dagger Starting Positions

Within the Primoris training system we will use the following Posta combinations as standard starting positions. This is purely to help with the illustration of techniques and, in reality, you should make yourself familiar with the actual names of the Posta being used.

Starting Position 1.
Red is in Tutta Porta di Ferro Sempia (Full Iron Door Single) opposing Green in Mezza Porta di Ferro Dopia Incrosada (Middle Iron Door Doubled and Crossed). ►

Starting Position 2.
Red is in Mezza Porta di Ferro Dopia (Middle Iron Door Doubled) opposing Green in Mezza Porta di Ferro Dopia Incrosada (Middle Iron Door Doubled and Crossed). ►

Starting Position 3.
Both Red and Green are in Mezza Porta di Ferro Dopia Incrosada (Middle Iron Door Doubled and Crossed) opposing each other. ►

Dagger Starting Positions

(Continued from previous page)

Starting Position 4.
Both Red and Green are in Mezza Porta di Ferro Dopia (Middle Iron Door Doubled) opposing each other. ►

Starting Position 5.
Red is in Tutta Porta di Ferro Dopia (Full Iron Door Doubled) opposing Green in Mezza Porta di Ferro Dopia (Middle Iron Door Doubled). ►

Starting Position 6.
Red is in Tutta Porta di Ferro Sempia (Full Iron Door Single) opposing Green in Mezza Porta di Ferro Dopia (Middle Iron Door Doubled). ►

Starting position 1

First Master Dagger Remedy

Left handed stop of high stab attack

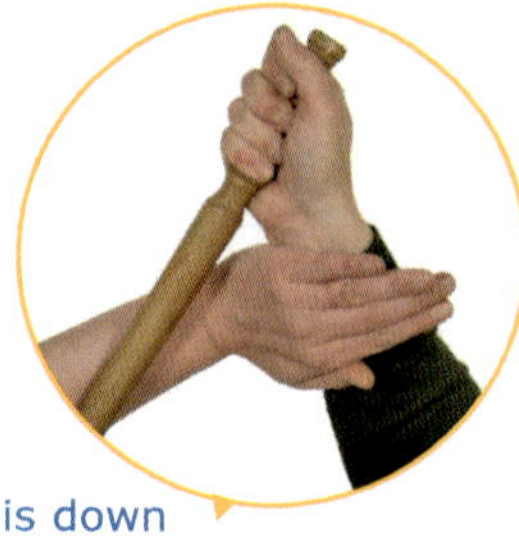

Note the thumb is down and a triangle is formed

See Unarmed for Posta Longa

Red defends from Green's incoming strike by stepping offline and coming up into Posta Longa under the dagger. Red's right hand is brought up ready for an immediate strike. ▶

Red's left hand rotates anti-clockwise taking the dagger outwards to start a disarm. Red's right hand is brought in for a hammer blow at the same time, using the hips to make the rotation to power both the disarm and strike. ◀

Red finishes the technique with the dagger being stripped from Green and a hammer blow counter strike. Note: that the counter strike could have also been made with a weapon, such as a dagger. ▶

Second Master Dagger Remedy

Cross armed stop of high stab attack

Starting position 1

Both arms are used to stop a strong incoming strike. This must be done by stepping offline enough that the dagger will not strike due to the shorter defending distance. The right arm is vertical supporting the horizontal left arm from behind. ◀

Red's left hand takes control of Green's wrist, in a thumb down position. Red's right arm cycles under Green's arm to come up and behind into a grip. ▶

The technique is completed by rotating Green's arm over Red's right arm, causing rotational damage to Green's shoulder. ◀

Third Master Dagger Remedy

Right handed stop of high stab attack

Starting position 1

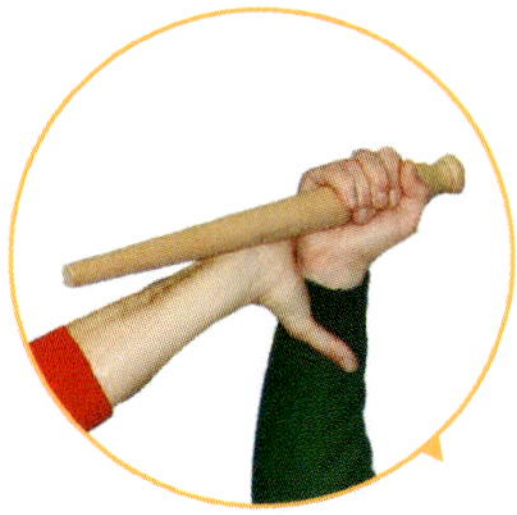

It is important that the feet are exchanged quickly so that right foot is leading and you have come offline. In later levels we will look at the, easier, lines of attack that do not require the feet to be exchanged. ▲

With the right foot now leading the right hand is used to stop the incoming strike by coming up into Posta Longa under the dagger. Note that the thumb is down. ►

See Unarmed for Posta Longa

The right arm is rotated clockwise and backwards extending the attackers arm out and pulling him off balance. The left hand immediately strikes at the attacker's elbow to damage, straighten and lock the arm. Note that Red is coming into Porta di Ferro. ◄

See Unarmed for Porta di Ferro

A Tutta Volta – full turn – is now used to force the attacker down to ground whilst retaining control of the attacker's right arm for follow-up damage. The Tutta Volta ensures that all the power comes from the legs and hips. ►

Third Master Dagger Remedy (alternate play)

Right Handed stop of high stab attack

Starting position 1

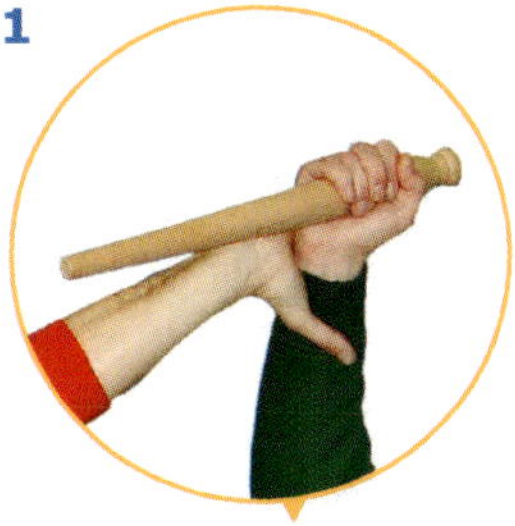

Again the right feet are exchanged. Later levels will introduce easier lines of attack that do not require the feet to be exchanged. ▲

Again the right foot is now leading and the right hand is used, thumb down, to stop the incoming attack. The right hand is then immediately brought down, with the momentum of the attack, to extend the attacker's arm past the defender. ◀

Red lets go of Green's wrist and strikes up with his forearm into the attacker's throat, whilst stepping behind the attacker with a Mezza Volta. This puts Red into the ideal position to perform a hip throw on Green. ▶

Fourth Master Dagger Remedy

Two handed stop of high stab attack

Starting position 1

Both hands are used, thumbs up, to stop the powerful incoming attack. This is a very good flinch defence reaction to the attack. ▶

The left hand is used to pull Green's arm down whilst, at the same time, the right hand is placed on the dagger blade to push it up. ◀

The combination of pulling Green's arm down and pushing the dagger upwards disarms Green and leaves Red ready for a thrust strike back at the attacker. ▶

Fifth Master Dagger Remedy (high threat)

Dealing with a grab attack and a threat from a dagger

Starting position 1

Green grabs hold of Red and creates a threat with his dagger. ▶

Red ignores the grab and immediately uses one of the dagger remedy plays to counter Green. In this example Red is using First Master Dagger Remedy. ◀

The key to this play is that Green also created a threat with the dagger when he grabbed onto Red. In this situation the grab has to be ignored and the dagger threat dealt with. Green is still at a disadvantage though, as Red can perform the majority of the dagger remedy plays without hindrance. Green has simply "given away" a weapon in the form of his left hand.

Fifth Master Dagger Remedy (low threat)

Dealing with a grab attack with minimum threat from the dagger

Starting position 1

Green grabs onto Red but is not creating an immediate threat with his dagger. ►

Red immediately uses one of the Abrazare plays to counter Green. ◄

The key to this play is that Green did not create a threat when he grabbed onto Red. In fact he gave Red his left arm without any real advantage to himself. In this situation Green's arm can be immediately attacked.

Sixth Master Dagger Remedy (inside)

Inside dagger stop of high dagger attack

Starting position 2

It is important that the feet are exchanged quickly so that right foot is leading and you have come offline. ▲

The dagger is used to stop a strong incoming attack on the inside of the attacker. This is done by swapping the feet and stepping offline enough, to the inside, that the dagger will not strike due to the shorter defending distance. Note that Red is now in an Abrazare Posta Frontale. ◄

Red then clears Green's dagger by pushing on Green's wrist in a manner similar to the immediate Posta Longa strike used in First Master Dagger Remedy. This then leaves Red clear to counter attack with a thrust to the Green's face or neck. ►

Sixth Master Dagger Remedy (outside)

Outside dagger stop of high dagger attack

Starting position 2

The dagger is used to stop a strong incoming attack on the outside of Green. This is done by stepping offline enough, to the outside, that Green's dagger will not strike due to the shorter defending distance. ◂

The play is completed by pushing at Green's elbow to both unbalance Green and to free the Red's dagger. Red is then clear to counter attack with a thrust to Green's face or neck. ▸

Seventh Master Dagger Remedy (inside)

Inside crossed dagger stop
of high dagger attack

Starting position 3

It is important that the feet are exchanged quickly so that right foot is leading and you have come offline. ▲

The crossed dagger is used to stop a strong incoming attack on the inside of Green. This is done by swapping the feet and stepping offline enough, to the inside, that the dagger will not strike due to the shorter defending distance. Note that due to the crossed defending dagger this defending distance is very short and normally this should be done with head protection. ◄

Red then clears Green's dagger by pushing on Green's wrist in a manner similar to the immediate Posta Longa strike used in First Master Dagger Remedy. This then leaves Red clear to counter attack with a stab to Green's face or neck. ►

Seventh Master Dagger Remedy (outside)

Outside crossed dagger stop of high dagger attack

Starting position 3

The crossed dagger is used to stop a strong incoming attack on the outside of Green. This is done by stepping offline enough, to the outside, that the dagger will not strike due to the shorter defending distance. Note that due to the crossed defending dagger this defending distance is very short and normally this should be done with head protection. ►

The play is completed by Red pushing at Green's elbow to both unbalance Green and to free Red's dagger. Red is then clear to counter attack with a stab to Green's face or neck. ◄

Eighth Master Dagger Remedy (armed)

Dagger stop of a low dagger thrust

Starting position 4

As this is a low thrust stab by Green, Red must give way to make distance with his body. Red's dagger is used in both hands to directly stop the incoming thrust. This also has the advantage of potentially causing damage to Green's wrist. The stop must be on the wrist, otherwise the attack may slip under Red's dagger and break through to strike home. ▲

Immediately Red sweeps Green's dagger arm out of the way and counters with his own thrust. ▲

Starting position 5

Eighth Master Dagger Remedy (unarmed)

Unarmed stop of a low dagger thrust

This is a difficult defence to master at speed, but it is very strong. Red comes offline to the inside of Green and makes full use of Tutta Porta di Ferro Double Posta to stop the incoming thrust. Using two hands makes this a very strong stop, but the distance of the dagger to the defender's body is very short, which is why it is very important to come offline. ▲

Red now rotates his left arm in an a clockwise motion bringing his left hand up to touch his own heart. This move will rotate Green's arm, turning his body and trapping the dagger, allowing for a quick strip of the dagger – which can be helped by a small Volta Stabile if necessary. ▲

Ninth Master Dagger Remedy

Unarmed stop of a low dagger thrust

Starting position 6

Against this low thrust stab, Red must give way to make distance with his body. Red uses both hands to directly stop the incoming thrust and to grab Green's forearm. Red's left hand should be on Green's wrist, with the right hand immediately above it. ►

Red keeps his left hand grip on Green's wrist to control it and uses his right hand to grab the dagger. The dagger is then rotated downwards and around, which will strip it from Green. ◄

Having stripped the dagger, Red then immediately thrusts back at Green. If this was a sharp-edged dagger then a tight grip will prevent Red from cutting his own hand. ►

Dagger Drills

Drilling is very important as a way to condition your body into becoming natural with the basic moves and applications of actual techniques. Techniques themselves cannot be trained in isolation as they will only give you a single, conditioned, response. This is why drilling is so important.

There are a lot of dagger drills available, but within Primoris we concentrate on three drills. You may wish to expand upon these drills yourself, but remember to try and stay as close to movements and practices that are correct for the techniques you are drilling.

The Basic High Drill is good for both attacker and defender. The attacker gets to practise different lines of high attacks and the defender gets to practise a quick response to these attacks. This is the same with the Basic Low Drill.

The Master Flow Drill will bring your training of the Master Remedies together and is an excellent way to both learn the Remedies and to keep movement, footwork and turning within your practice.

Basic High Attack Dagger Drill

This is a basic dagger drill for practising defence against high attacks using three Masters of Dagger. It is a repetitious drill and the attacker can introduce variety in the combinations as the defender improves in skill and speed.

Both are in Starting Position 1 for dagger versa unarmed Postas - Tutta Porta di Ferro Sempia for the defender and Mezza Porta di Ferro Dopia Incrosada for the attacker. ▲

The attacker uses Mezza Volta footwork to make the attack to the right. The defender uses First Master Dagger Remedy to stop the attack. ▲

Basic High Attack Dagger Drill

(Continued from previous page)

Both reset back to the original Posta positions. This reset should be quick to keep the flow of the drill moving. ▲

The attacker uses Mezza Volta footwork to make the attack down the centre. The defender uses Fourth Master Dagger Remedy to stop the attack. ▲

Basic High Attack Dagger Drill

(Continued from previous page)

Both reset back to the original Posta positions. Again this needs to be a quick reset. ▲

The attacker uses Mezza Volta footwork to make the attack to the left. The defender uses Third Master Dagger Remedy to stop the attack. ▲

The drill then repeats.

Basic Low Attack Dagger Drill

This is a basic dagger drill for practising defence against low attacks using the principles of the Eighth and Ninth Masters of Dagger. It is a repetitious drill and the attacker can introduce variety in the combinations as the defender improves in skill and speed.

The attacker starts in Mezza Porta di Ferro Dopia and the defender starts in an upright standing position for the best use of this drill. ▲

The attacker uses Mezza Volta footwork to make a thrust attack to the right. The defender gives ground and sweeps the strike out of the way with the left arm using the principles of Eighth Master Dagger Remedy. ▲

Basic Low Attack Dagger Drill

(Continued from previous page)

Both reset back to the original starting positions. This should be a quick reset to keep the flow of the drill moving. ▲

The attacker uses Mezza Volta footwork to make a thrust attack down the centre. The defender gives ground and stops the strike using Ninth Master Dagger Remedy. ▲

Basic Low Attack Dagger Drill

(Continued from previous page)

Both reset back to the original starting positions. Again this should be a quick reset. ▲

The attacker uses Mezza Volta footwork to make a thrust attack to the left. The defender gives ground and sweeps the strike out of the way with the right arm using the principles of Eighth Master Dagger Remedy. ▲

The drill then repeats.

Dagger Master Flow Drill

This drill takes both students through eight of the nine Dagger Masters. The fifth Master is ignored, at this stage, as it involves the attacking student grabbing the other student's neck area and so can break the flow of the drill.

The idea behind the drill is to build up slowly into a faster flow and this will enable the defending student to build a more natural knowledge of the Dagger Masters. It is important that the drill is built up – the idea is to assist the defender in learning, not to deliberately catch him or her out.

The attacker gets to practise making good, smooth and consistent attacks with the dagger. Once the drill has been performed a few times then the students should swap the roles of attacker and defender.

In the following illustrations Red will be the defender and Green will be the attacker. Only the initial defence of each Dagger Master is used at this level of training – the drill is expanded upon within Secundus and later levels.

Begin in Starting Position 1. Red is in Tutta Porta di Ferro Sempia (Full Iron Door Single) and Green is in Mezza Porta di Ferro Dopia Incrosada (Middle Iron Door Doubled and Crossed). ▲

Green attacks and Red performs the First Master Dagger Remedy. ▲

Both students reset back to Starting Position 1. ▲

Green attacks and Red performs the Second Master Dagger Remedy. ▲

Dagger Master Flow Drill

(Continued from previous page)

Both students reset back to Starting Position 1. ▲

Green attacks and Red performs the Third Master Dagger Remedy. ▲

Both students reset back to Starting Position 1. ▲

Green attacks and Red performs the Fourth Master Dagger Remedy. ▲

Reset to Starting Position 2. Red collects his own training Dagger (from a belt or waste band) and resets back to Mezza Porta di Ferro Dopia (Middle Iron Door Doubled). Green resets, staying in Mezza Porta di Ferro Dopia Incrosada (Middle Iron Door Doubled and Crossed). ▲

Green attacks and Red performs the Sixth Master Dagger Remedy. ▲

Dagger Master Flow Drill

(Continued from previous page)

Reset to Starting Position 3. Red reverses the hold on his Dagger as he resets into Mezza Porta di Ferro Dopia Incrosada (Middle Iron Door Doubled and Crossed), which is now the same position as Green. ▲

Green attacks and Red performs the Seventh Master Dagger Remedy on the inside. ▲

Change to Starting Position 5. Red resets into Tutta Porta di Ferro Dopia (Full Iron Door Doubled). Green reverses the hold on his Dagger and resets into Mezza Porta di Ferro Dopia (Middle Iron Door Doubled). ▲

Green attacks and Red performs the unarmed Eighth Master Dagger Remedy. ▲

Change to Starting Position 6. Red resets into Tutta Porta di Ferro Sempia (Full Iron Door Single). Green resets back into Mezza Porta di Ferro Dopia (Middle Iron Door Doubled). ▲

Green attacks and Red performs the unarmed Ninth Master Dagger Remedy. ▲

Both students will now reset back to Starting Position 1 and repeat the flow drill.

Introduction to Sword (Spada)

In Primoris we focus on the use of the sword one handed. This approach gives the basis behind which the rest of the sword system can be built upon in later levels and links to both the unarmed and the dagger.

It must be remembered that Fiore created a single integrated system, so that different weapons introduce variations in the application of common techniques.

Within the Primoris sword section you will be shown all of the principle techniques required for a single handed sword fight by learning how to correctly use the sword for attack and defence. The principles shown, when taken in conjunction with footwork and turning, will show you how to defend with covers, beats and breaks; to correctly form fighting postas; as guards and positions; perform attacks both correctly and down the best lines and this is brought together with some practice drills.

Keeping within the context of the Fiore system you will be shown how to use the sword, one handed, to the level of Master Battle. This is a very important, fundamental, point to reach as all of the other sword Masters and techniques require that you fully understand and are competent at Master Battle.

Sword Fundamentals

It is important with any system that you understand the fundamentals involved. This is not any different with using a sword.

This section will describe three fundamentals – the sword itself; the single handed sword postas and the importance of distance with the sword. Other fundamentals, such as how to cut correctly; footwork and turning; throws; falling; etc. are contained within their own sections, but are of equal importance.

One of the main aims of Primoris is to give you the grounding required to fully apply and understand the Martial Art of Fiore. To this end you must understand the weapon that you are using and how it is constructed. Different parts of the sword will be used in different ways and have different characteristics; correctly using posta fighting positions will allow your brain to find the most advantageous positions from which you can use the sword with the minimum of thought and knowing the correct use of sword distance is vital for both your attack and defence.

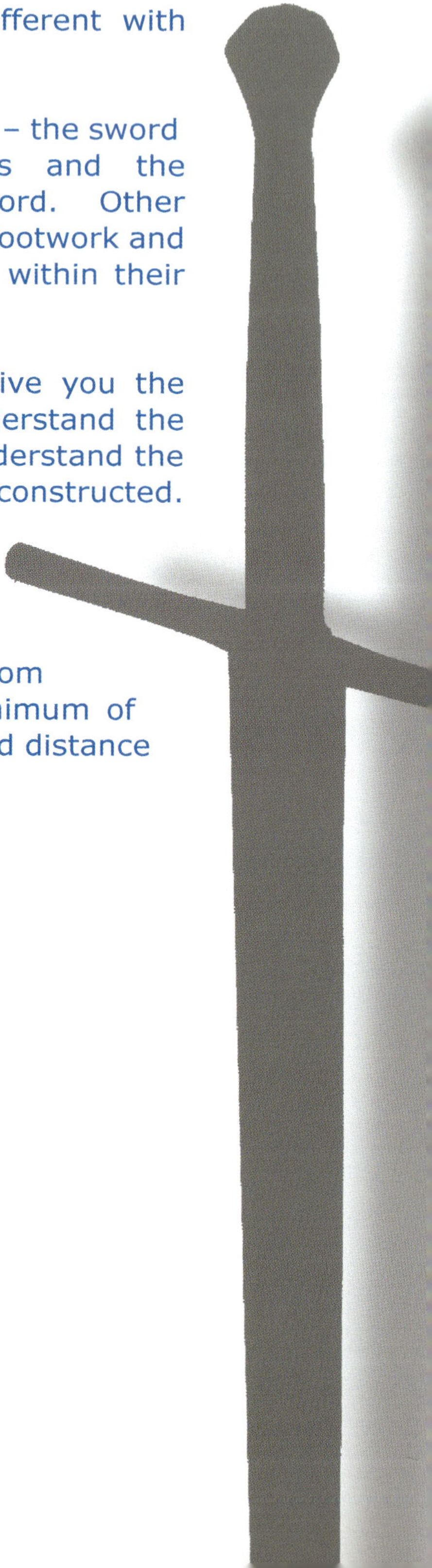

The Sword

The sword is not as simple a weapon as you might initially think. It is defined in several different sections that each have their own uses and it is important that you understand this weapon so that you can employ it to your maximum benefit.

Here we are discussing a Hand-and-half or Longsword that is designed to be held in one or two hands.

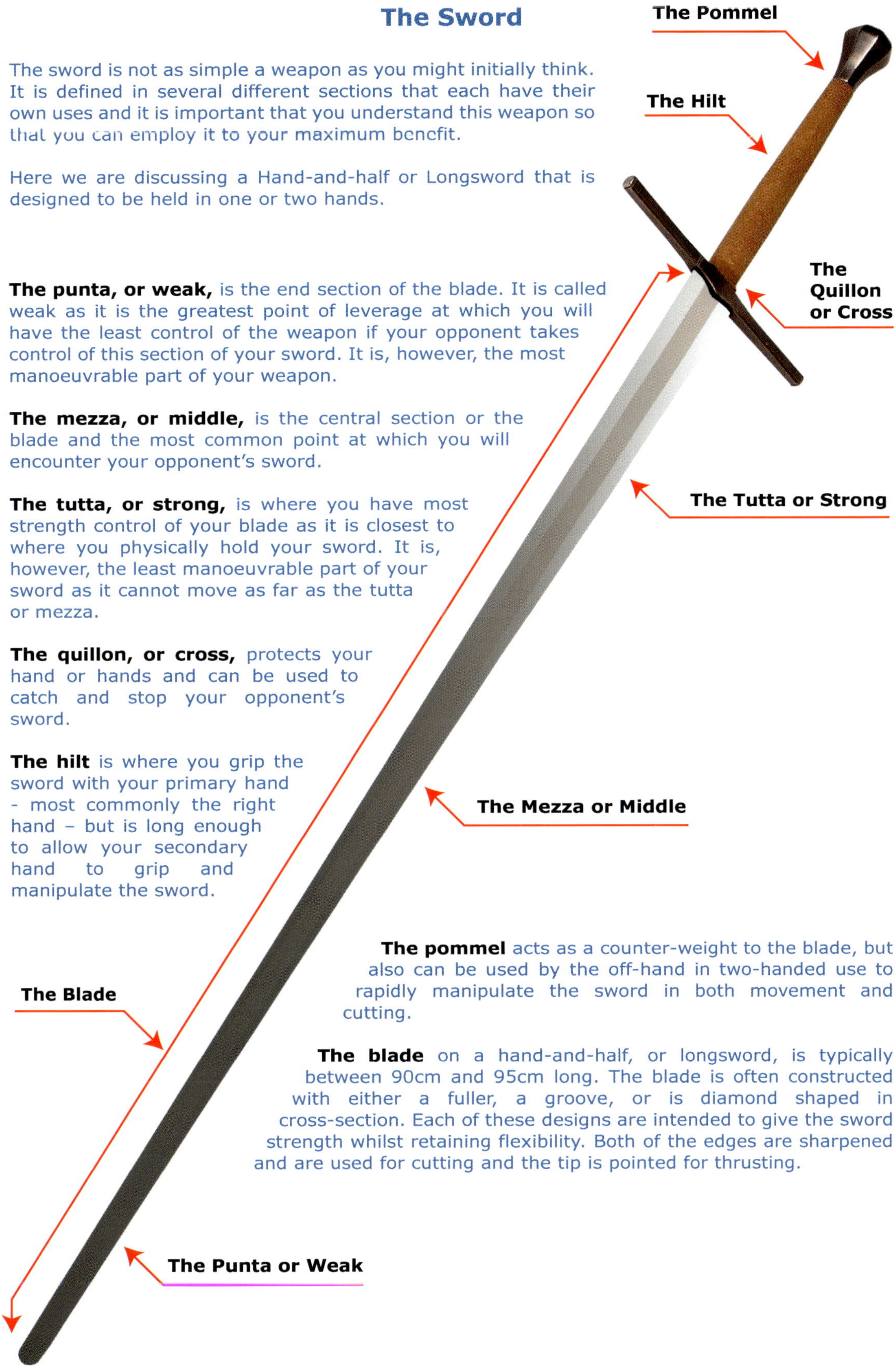

The punta, or weak, is the end section of the blade. It is called weak as it is the greatest point of leverage at which you will have the least control of the weapon if your opponent takes control of this section of your sword. It is, however, the most manoeuvrable part of your weapon.

The mezza, or middle, is the central section or the blade and the most common point at which you will encounter your opponent's sword.

The tutta, or strong, is where you have most strength control of your blade as it is closest to where you physically hold your sword. It is, however, the least manoeuvrable part of your sword as it cannot move as far as the tutta or mezza.

The quillon, or cross, protects your hand or hands and can be used to catch and stop your opponent's sword.

The hilt is where you grip the sword with your primary hand - most commonly the right hand – but is long enough to allow your secondary hand to grip and manipulate the sword.

The pommel acts as a counter-weight to the blade, but also can be used by the off-hand in two-handed use to rapidly manipulate the sword in both movement and cutting.

The blade on a hand-and-half, or longsword, is typically between 90cm and 95cm long. The blade is often constructed with either a fuller, a groove, or is diamond shaped in cross-section. Each of these designs are intended to give the sword strength whilst retaining flexibility. Both of the edges are sharpened and are used for cutting and the tip is pointed for thrusting.

The Sword

(Continued from previous page)

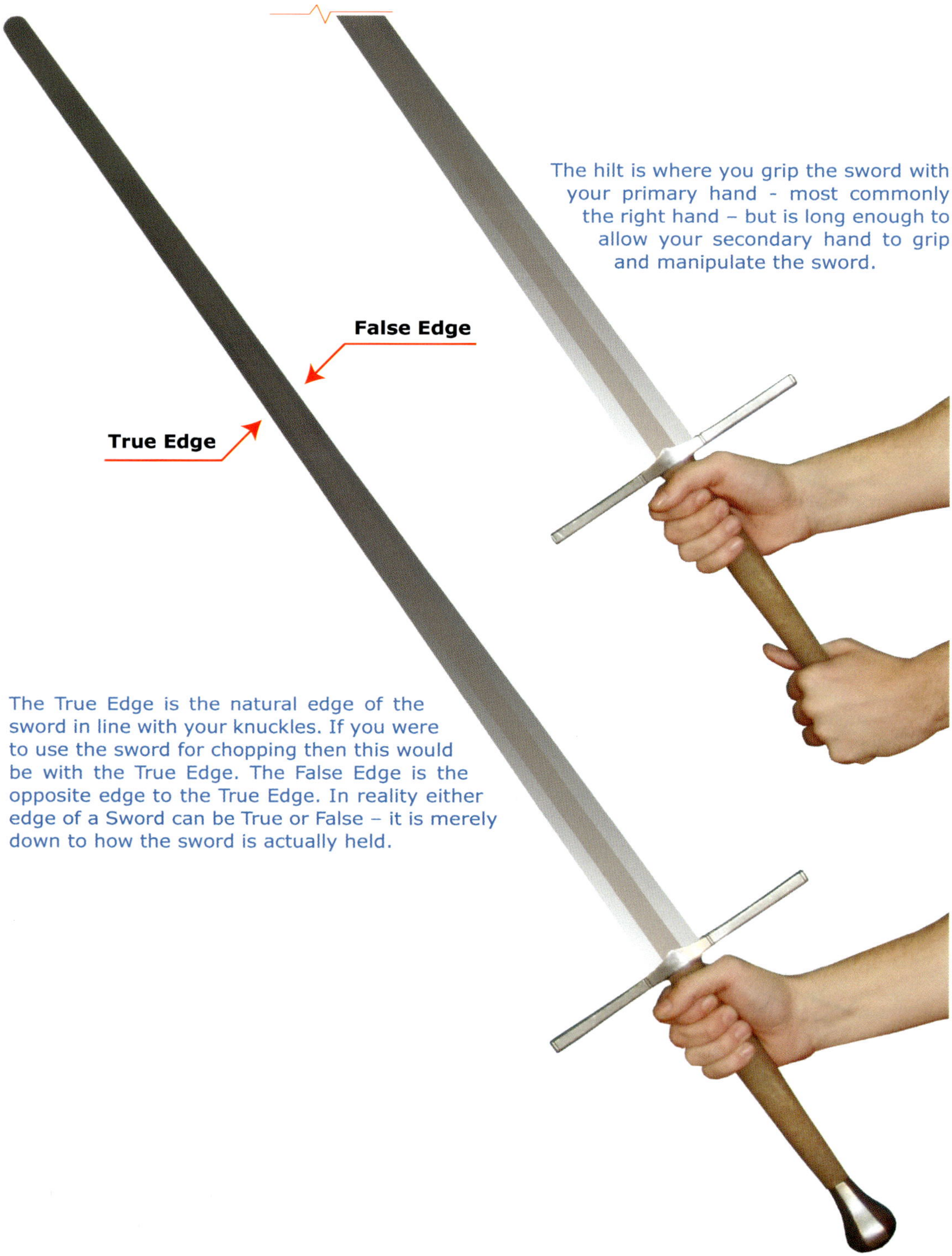

The hilt is where you grip the sword with your primary hand - most commonly the right hand – but is long enough to allow your secondary hand to grip and manipulate the sword.

The True Edge is the natural edge of the sword in line with your knuckles. If you were to use the sword for chopping then this would be with the True Edge. The False Edge is the opposite edge to the True Edge. In reality either edge of a Sword can be True or False – it is merely down to how the sword is actually held.

Sword Distance

This illustrates a very important principle of sword fighting that is often misrepresented in other media. It would appear, to Green, that Red's leading leg is exposed and that it is possible for him to make a quick cut at the exposed leg, ending the engagement. ►

Green has performed a Mezza Volta and has tried a low cut at Red's leg. Red simply withdraws his leading leg and responds with a Fendente to Green's head. Even if Red had not withdrawn his leg then the Fendente response would have caused more damage and could well have forced Green to abandon his attack and try to respond to Red's cut.

It is important to understand that the legs are an opportunistic target only, never an opening target. It is easy to see that Red has a much shorter distance to reach Green's head than Green has to reach Red's leg. ◄

This shows a starting position that is incorrect. Both combatants are too close to each other and it is a gamble as to who will be the quickest to make a quick strike or exploit an opening. Always ideally start an engagement out of distance, so that you either have to step in behind your own attack or your opponent must step to you to make his or her attack.

Being out of distance does not mean that you cannot strike your opponent, rather that they cannot strike you without one of you stepping towards the other. Obviously if you have a long reach – due to arm or weapon length – and can hit your opponent then this is to your advantage, even though you may be out of distance to their strike. ►

Single Handed Sword Posta

There are only really three sword Posta positions used at this level, none of which are actually named by Fiore.

This is a high position to the right. It is mainly used for Covers to the right and Breaks to the left as well as Fendente and Mezani cuts from the right and high Punte thrusts. ▸

This is a low position to the right. It is mainly used for Beats from the right and Covers on the left as well as Fendente cuts from the right and Punte thrusts. ◂

This is a low position to the left and is the most powerful starting position for single handed sword use. It can perform Covers to the left and right, Beats from the left and Breaks to the right against cuts, thrusts and thrown swords. It can make the most versatile of the positions. Fendente, Mezani and Sottani cuts from the left; low Punte thrusts and opportunistic Fendente cuts from the right. ▴

Sword Cuts

The ability to cut correctly with the sword is both vital and fundamental to the correct use of the weapon.

Sword cutting seems to be obvious, but it is a necessary skill that has to be mastered. Within Primoris we concentrate on two main elements – the physical way to perform a cut and the best lines that a cut can take.

Technically a thrust is not a cut, but it is a blow and so is included in this section. All cuts, or blows, are called colpi. In total there are seven colpi, blows, that need to be learned:.

- **Two Fendente angled downward cuts, one from each side.**
- **Two Sottani angled upward cuts, one from each side.**
- **Two Mezani horizontal cuts, one from each side.**
- **The Punte thrust.**

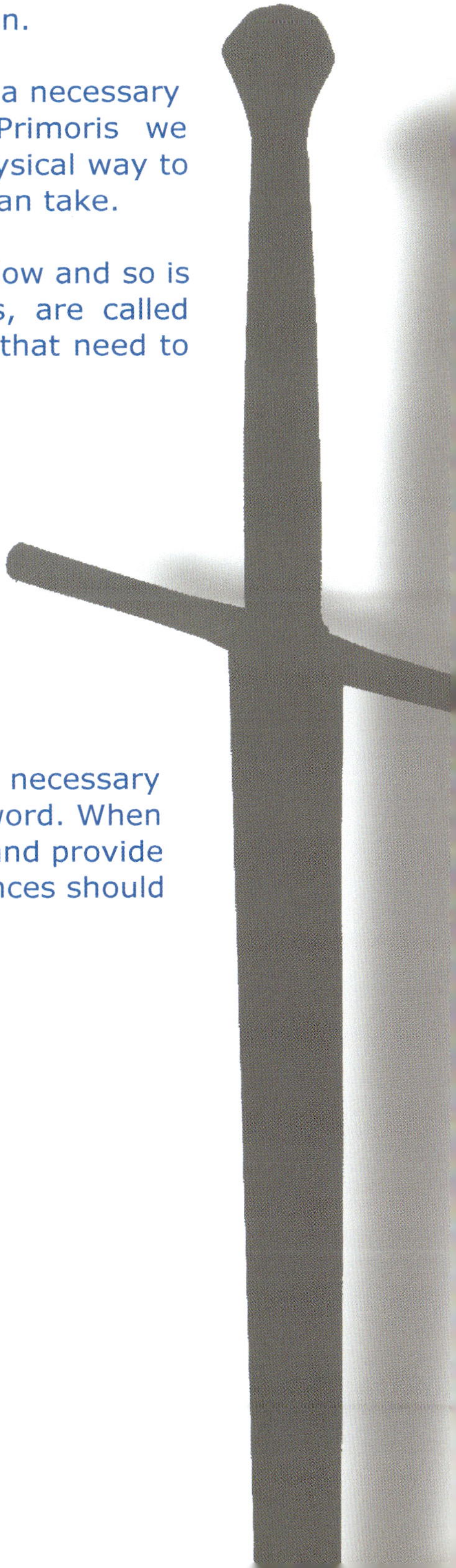

These colpi blows together give all of the necessary lines of attack that you will require with a sword. When correctly applied they will both protect you and provide the threats that all of your attacks and defences should incorporate.

How to Cut

The technique of cutting with a sword is very important and, correctly done, will generate a more powerful, accurate cut whilst maintaining a better defence. It is easy for anyone to pick up a sword and cut with it, but many people will find that they have been struck by their opponent before their own cut has landed.

In this example we start from a high position on the right and will perform a Fendente cut. Power needs to be generated from the hips and legs, which contain the largest muscles in the body.

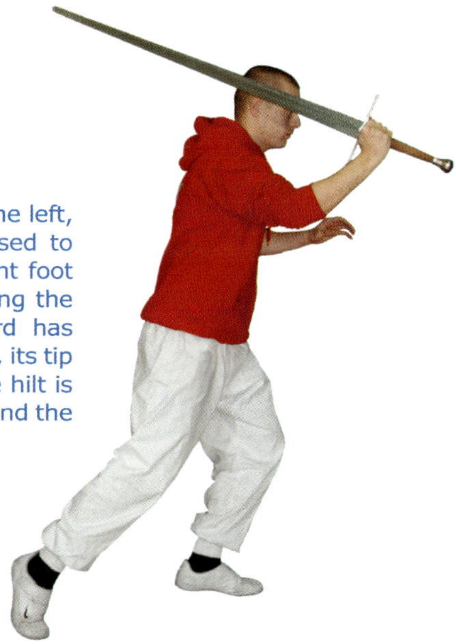

An accrease with the left foot, to the left, allows the hips and legs to be used to generate power. Note how the right foot pivots as part of the hip twist giving the maximum momentum. The sword has not really been moved at this point, its tip is still trailing behind, although the hilt is coming forward with the hip twist and the right arm.

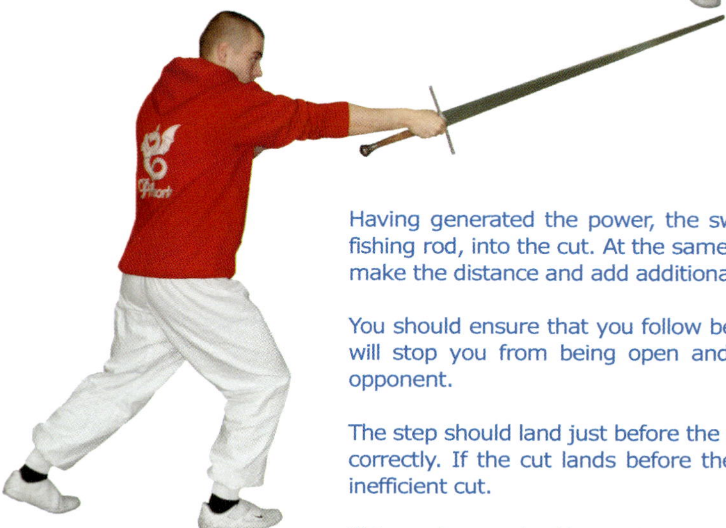

Having generated the power, the sword then whips out, like casting a fishing rod, into the cut. At the same time a Mezza Volta step is taken to make the distance and add additional power.

You should ensure that you follow behind the sword, as you cut, as this will stop you from being open and create a constant threat to your opponent.

The step should land just before the cut makes contact if you are cutting correctly. If the cut lands before the step is completed then this is an inefficient cut.

This can be practiced by cutting at a pell or some other target and making sure that you foot lands before you hear the sword contact.

Fendente

Downward Cut

The Fendente is a downward cut. It is not vertical, but at an angle and can be done from the right and from the left. The angle, though, must be steep otherwise the attacker will leave themselves open for easy counters to the strike.

The path of the Fendente should take a line from the side of the opponent's mouth through to the knee on the opposite side from the cut.

Within Primoris this cut is always done with the true edge of the sword and is in the opposite direction to the Sottani cut.

This is the path of a Fendente from the left. ◄

This is the path of a Fendente from the right. ►

The Fendente cut from the left. ▲

The Fendente cut from the right. ▲

Example of the right leg finish on the Fendente cut from the right. ▲

To generate the maximum power with the hips and to get the longest cutting distance it is always best to finish with the same leg leading on the side from which you are cutting – right leg lead for a right side cut and left leg lead for a left side cut – regardless of whether you are cutting with a step forwards or backwards.

Cutting with a leg leading on the opposite side is called cross-cutting.

Sottani

Upward Cut

The Sottani is an upward cut. It is a steeply angled cut that can be done from the left and from the right.

The path of the Sottani should take a line from the opponent's knee, on the same side as the cut, up through the side of their mouth on the opposite side from the cut.

This cut is normally done with the false edge of the sword, although sometimes it can be done with the true edge as part of a cover or a quick snipe. The Sottani is in the opposite direction to the Fendente cut.

This is the path of a Sottani from the left. ◄

The Sottani cut from the left. ▲

This is the path of a Sottani from the right. ►

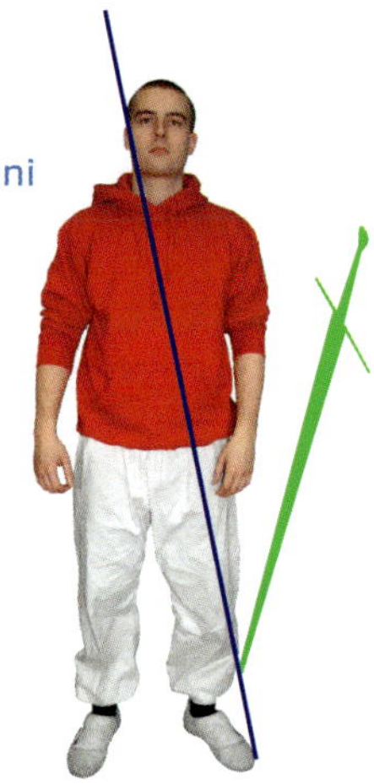

The Sottani cut from the right. ▲

To generate the maximum power with the hips and to get the longest cutting distance it is normally best to finish with the same leg leading on the side from which you are cutting - right leg lead for a right side cut and left leg lead for a left side cut - regardless of whether you are cutting with a step forwards or backwards.

Cutting with a leg leading on the opposite side is called cross-cutting and can be effective when you need to cut quickly - i.e. Where you already have distance and a step would not give any advantage.

This is a quick cross-cut Sottani. ▲

Mezani

Horizontal Cut

The Mezani is a horizontal cut that can be done from the left and from the right. A Mezani can be made as a cut anywhere from the knees up to the head.

From the right this cut is always done with the true edge and from the left it is always done with the false edge. A true edge cut from your left may feel natural, but is it wrong as it requires the wrist to be turned and also means that the cut will lead with the hand, rather than the sword.

Example of an incorrect method of cutting from the left with a true edge lead. Note how the hand is leading the cut and so is very vulnerable. ►

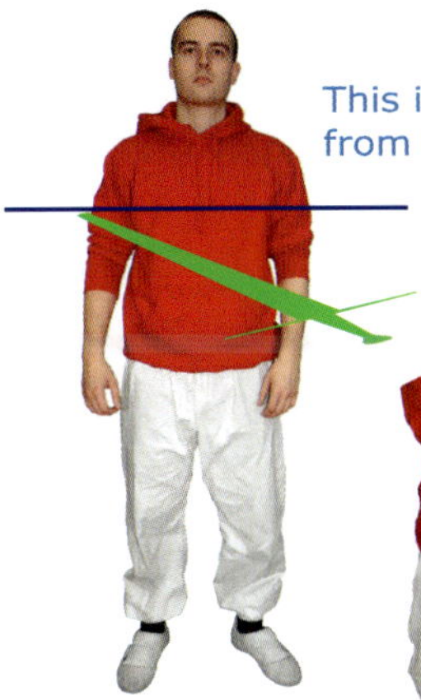

This is the path of a Mezani from the left. ◄

This is the path of a Meza from the right. ►

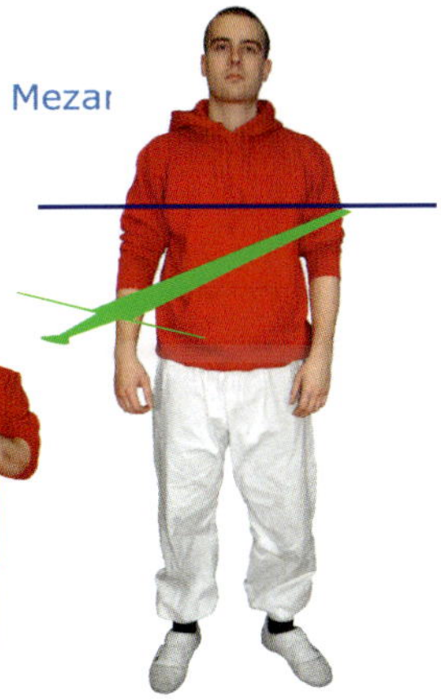

The Mezani cut from the left. ▲

The Mezani cut from the right. ▲

To generate the maximum power with the hips and to get the longest cutting distance it is always best to finish with the same leg leading on the side from which you are cutting – right leg lead for a right side cut and left leg lead for a left side cut – regardless of whether you are cutting with a step forwards or backwards.

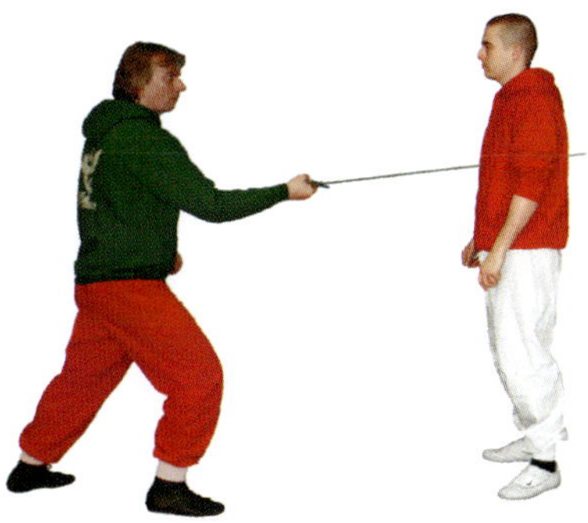

This is a quick cross-cut Mezani. ▲

Cutting with a leg leading on the opposite side is called cross-cutting and can be useful for quick attacks that do not require a closing of distance.

Punte

Thrust

The Punte is a thrust with the sword. It can be done high towards the throat or face or it can be done low towards the lower abdomen. Although this is a very effective attack it can be slow to recover from especially if done with a step forward, which is a problem if the Punte is Covered or countered by the opponent and they are beginning their counter attack.

To make the maximum use of thrusting distance, for a right handed Player, Punte is always best performed with a right leg finish, regardless of whether stepping forward or backwards.

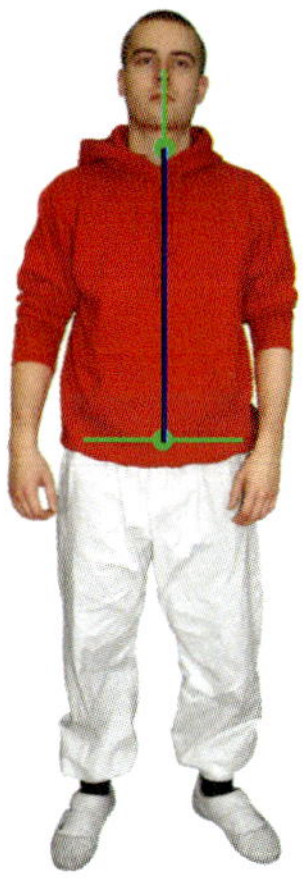

Low Punte thrust. Note the right leg finish. ▸

This shows the areas of attack for a Punte. ▴

High Punte thrust. Note the right leg finish. ▴

Example of a low Punte thrust. ▴

Example of a high Punte thrust. ▸

Sword Colpi

Here we see the vertical lines of attack for Fendente (downwards) and Sottani (upwards) cuts; the horizontal Mezani line of attack cut, which could be anywhere from the lower abdomen to the head and the centre line showing that the Punte thrust can be made between the abdomen and the head.

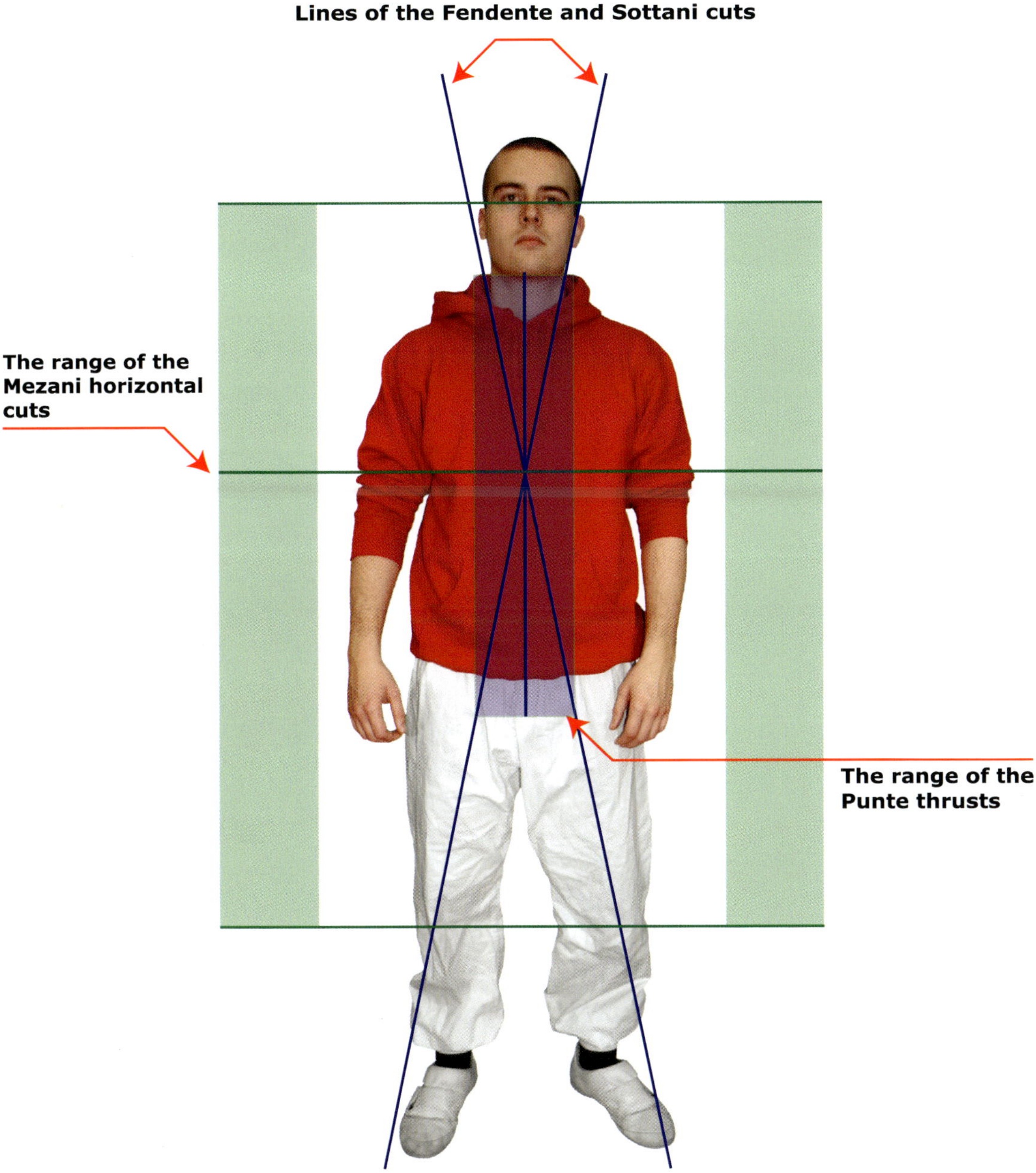

Safe Cutting with the Sword

It is important that you learn how to cut safely with the sword. Although the martial aspect of the art is to damage your opponent, we do not want this to happen within training. By learning how to control your sword you will be able to place your attacks safely and you will be able to pull your attacks if your training partner is in an unexpected position where they may get injured. This practice can be done solo with a pell or any form or barrier, but here we will show how this is done with a training partner.

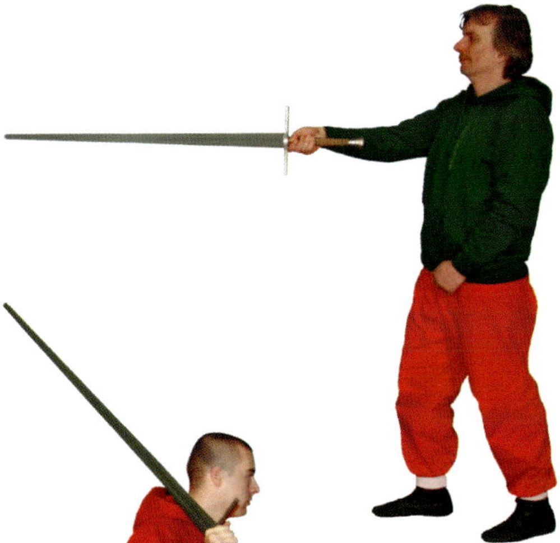

Your training partner holds out their sword horizontally. You will perform each cut against this sword. ◄

As you cut you are looking to getting as close to your partner's sword as possible without actually striking it. If you do strike it then it should be a light strike only. Remember this could be flesh and bone in reality so we are looking for minimal damage, but you must strike at full force initially. ▼

This strike to too hard and has moved Green and his sword. This must not happen as this means Red's strike was too powerful and not under control. ◄

The strike was too hard

Sword Techniques

Within the Primoris sword section we concentrate on bringing you up to the stage of Master Battle with the sword in one hand. This means that together with the fundamentals of sword use, understanding, posta positions and guards, colpi blows, footwork, etc. you must apply the key areas of defence that allow for a rapid counter-attack or response.

The following techniques demonstrate how you can defend yourself against any incoming one handed sword attack and, expanded upon in later levels, against other form of sword and weapon attacks.

These techniques are crucial to all sword and weapon forms and cover three basic principles:

- **The cover, where you cover yourself again a potential attack.**
- **The beat, where you beat an attack out of the way.**
- **The break, where you break an attack with force.**

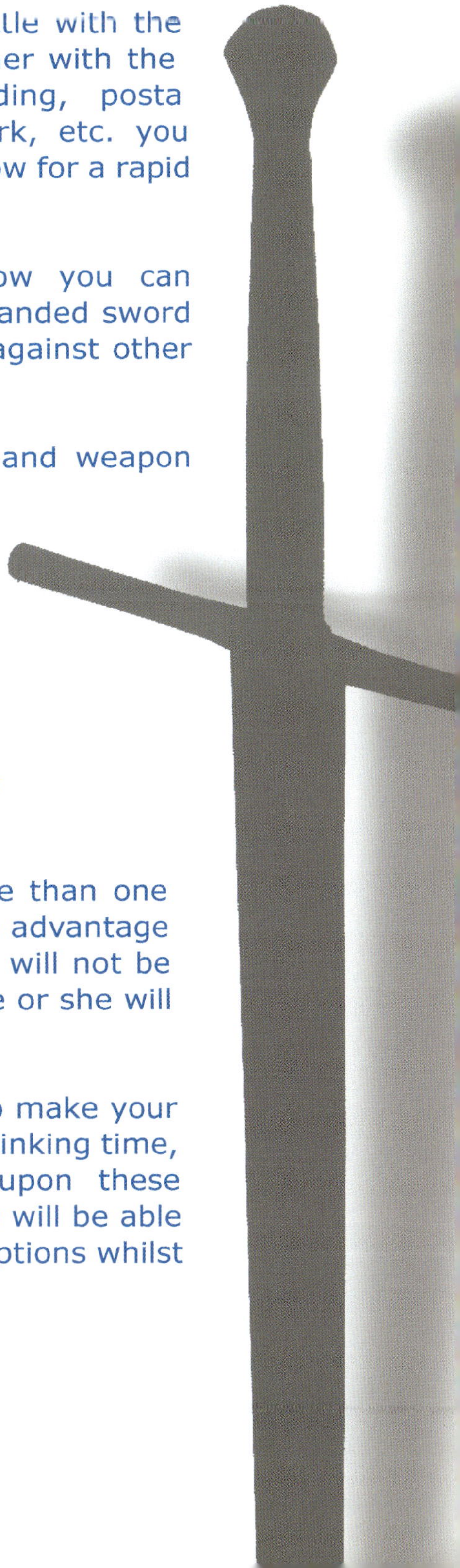

Collectively these techniques give you more than one option to oppose an opponent's attack. The advantage of having more than one option is that you will not be predictable to your opponent and, hence, he or she will not be able to easily counter your response.

By training these techniques you will able to make your response to an attack without the delay of thinking time, yet remain unpredictable. As we build upon these responses and techniques in later levels you will be able to expand your repertoire to increase your options whilst maintaining a minimal response time.

Inside Sword Cover

Left Leg Forward

This version of the inside Cover is performed with the left leg leading. It is important that the sword has the true edge upwards - not toward the incoming sword - as this leaves your sword ready for an immediate counter cut without any rotation of the wrist. The sword is also sloping backwards which will allow any contacting sword to slide off away from the body. ◄

Red starts with his sword low on the left and Green starts with his sword high on the right. ◄►

Red will perform the technique

As Green attacks, Red immediately accreases his front foot off to his right and steps through with a Mezza Volta. This brings him in deep to Green giving him several options. ▲

Inside Sword Cover

Left Leg Forward
(Continued from previous page)

Here, as well as stepping in with a Mezza Volta, Red has put his hand under the hilt of Green's sword. This is the same technique as used in the Dagger First Master Remedy and shows how the Dagger Plays can be used within the Sword Plays. ◄

Having cleared Green's sword out of the way, Red finishes off the technique bringing his own sword up to thrust in the same way that the Dagger version of the technique would use a hammer blow strike. ▲

In another example finish, Green has performed the technique with a deep cover and is using a Ligadura Mezana Play, which is also found in Dagger First Master Remedy. When fully applied, this bind will rotate Red's shoulder. ◄

Green shows an alternative finish

Inside Sword Cover

Right Leg Forward

This is a quick Cover to perform from the Low Left Posta position as it simply involves raising the sword arm whilst doing an Accrease to adjust the body position. It is important to note that the sword is raised with the true edge upwards – not toward the incoming sword – this leaves your sword ready for an immediate counter cut without any rotation of the wrist. The sword is also sloping backwards which will allow any contacting sword to slide off away from the body. ◀

Red will perform the technique

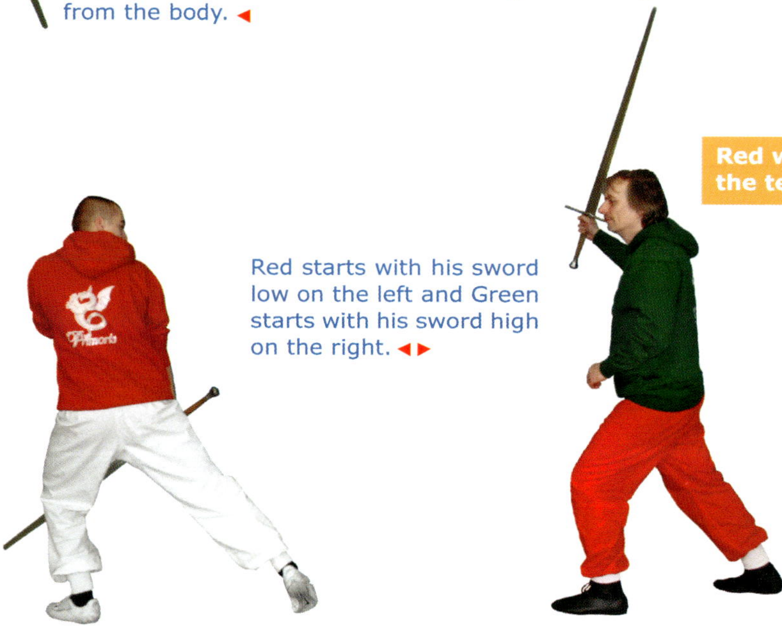

Red starts with his sword low on the left and Green starts with his sword high on the right. ◀▶

As Green attacks, Red immediately accreases his front foot off to his right and adjusts his body position as he brings his sword up to perform the cover. ▲

Outside Sword Cover

This is the basic Cover for an attack coming in to your right. You bring your sword to your right which will cover their sword off to your right, leaving their outside line open for an attack. This Cover can also be performed against attacks coming in to your left and is the basic Cover against a thrust. ◀

Red will perform the technique

Red starts with his sword low on the left and Green starts with his sword high on the right. ◀ ▶

Green starts a Fendente cut. Red accreases his front foot offline to his left. ▲

Outside Sword Cover

(Continued from previous page)

As Green finishes his Fendente cut, Red performs a Mezza Volta to step forward around the outside of Green's attack. If Red's footwork is accurate and fast then he will avoid any contact with Green's sword, but Red's sword is still there to cover if required. ▲

Red immediately counter attacks with his own cut. He could have used a Punte or moved in for a closer strike or grapple. ▲

Outside Sword Beat

The sword Beat is the deflection of an incoming Fendente or Mezani attack. It is very easy and effective, but can be difficult to master psychologically. This is the outside beat as it brings the defender to the outside of the attacker's sword.

Green will perform the technique

Red starts with high sword high to the right. Green, who will perform the technique starts with his sword low on the left. ▲

As Red starts to cut in with a Fendente attack, Green accreases off to his left. ▲

Outside Sword Beat

(Continued from previous page)

Green performs a full Sottani cut with a Mezza Volta step at an angle past Red's right. If Green's footwork has been fast and accurate then he will slip Red's Fendente cut and the swords will not contact. If the blades do contact then Green's Sottani cut will deflect Red's sword over Green's head.

It is vital that Green does not track or follow Red's sword with his own, which is a common mistake on this beat. If he does this then he will take his own sword off-line and leave himself open to another attack. All Green should do is a good Sottani cut as the technique will protect him. ▲

Green then counters with his own cut, stepping forward with a Mezza Volta.►

Outside Sword Beat Practise

The outside sword Beats can be difficult to master as they are not instinctive counters to incoming attacks, even though they only use standard footwork and cuts. This is a safety practice technique based around one training partner holding his sword out to allow for safe Beats until the technique is mastered.

Red starts in Single Sword Posta Low and Left. Green stands with his sword extended. ◄ ►

Red performs an outside Beat on Green's sword. ◄

The Beat is completed and Red is ready to counter strike. ►

Inside Sword Beat

The inside sword Beat, which brings the defender to the inside of the attacker's sword is very effective against a Fendente or Mezani attack to the defender's right when the defender's sword is low to his right. Again, this is an easy and effective technique, but a difficult one to master psychologically as it does not feel natural.

Red, who will perform the technique, starts with his sword low on the right and Green starts with his sword low on the left.▲

As Green starts his attack, where his sword will come over for a Fendente cut, Red accreases off to his right with his leading left foot.▲

Inside Sword Beat

(Continued from previous page)

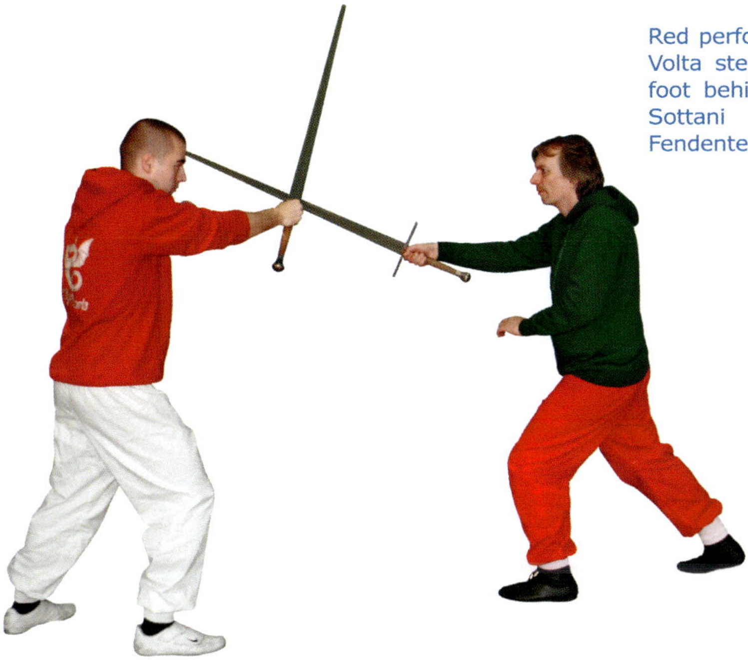

Red performs a full Sottani with a Mezza Volta step, finishing by drawing his left foot behind in a small Tutta Volta. The Sottani cut deflects the incoming Fendente off to Red's left.◄

It is vitally important that Red does not track or follow Green's sword with his own. The Sottani cut is enough to complete the technique and any form of tracking will just weaken Red's position, rather than having his sword ready for an immediate counter strike. ▲

Red counters with his own cut, stepping forward with a Mezza Volta.►

Inside Sword Beat Practise

This is a safe practice technique for the inside sword Beats, where one training partner holds his sword out to allow for safe Beats until the technique is mastered, which can be difficult as Beats arc not natural techniques.

Red starts in a Single Sword Posta low and Right. Green stands with his sword extended. ◄►

Red performs an inside beat on Green's sword ◄►

The beat is completed and Red is ready to counter strike. ◄►

Inside Break

An inside Break cuts down onto the incoming sword leaving you on the inside of the attacker. Although this is also a good technique against a Fendente cut, at this level it is normally used against a Mezani cut.

The Break is performed by stepping into the path of the incoming blade and making a full Fendente cut. This will smash the blade safely down and out of the way.

Red will perform the technique

Red and Green start with their swords high on the right. ◄ ►

Green attacks with a Mezani cut. Red accreases off to his left and begins his Fendente cut. ◄

Red performs a Mezza Volta, stepping into the path of the incoming blade, and completes his Fendente cut which strikes down onto Green's Mezani cut. Red can now counter-strike, for example with a Sottani at Green's head. ►

Outside Break

An outside Break is a cut down onto the incoming sword which leaves you on the outside of the attacker. Normally it is against an incoming Mezani cut, but it can also be done against a Fendente cut. In a real engagement it would also be legitimate to perform the break against the attacker's arm.

The break is performed by stepping into the path of the incoming blade and making a full Fendente cut. This will smash the blade safely down and out of the way.

Red will perform the technique

Both Players start with their swords down on the left. ▲

Green attacks with a Mezani cut. Red accreases off to his left and begins his Fendente cut. ◄

Red performs a Mezza Volta, stepping into the path of the incoming blade, and completes his Fendente cut which strikes down onto Green's Mezani cut. Red can now counter-strike, for example with a Sottani at Green's head. ►

Sword Drills

It is essential that you drill as this is the only way that you can condition your body into building upon the basic moves of actual techniques. Although techniques are vital, they cannot be trained in isolation as that will only condition you to a single response and a real engagement is normally a series of actions, responses and counter-responses.

Various sword drills exist, but at this level we introduce those that will allow you to practise the three main techniques that have been taught – the cover, the beat and the break. In addition to this you will be given a basic exercise flow drill.

The exercise drill, like all drills, is not intended to be a reflection of reality but rather to impart certain principles and movements. In this case movement and free flowing cuts are the most important aspect of the drill. As this drill builds up you will find that you are moving more and that your footwork is coming into synchronisation with your sword work. The more fluid the drill becomes the more your body will naturally follow the motions dictated by the sword. This is true of all drills and is the reason that drilling is important to any Martial Art.

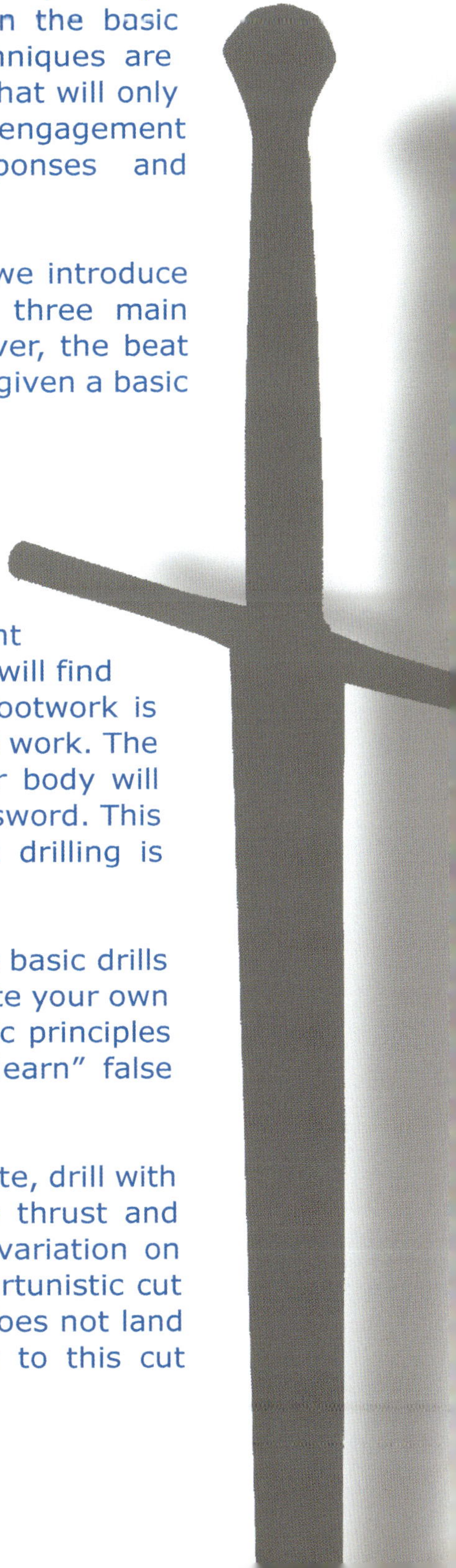

Do not feel that you must only stay with the basic drills that we supply at this level. Feel free to create your own drills, but remember to stay within the basic principles of the Art itself as you do not want to "learn" false techniques through drilling.

An example of this might be a thrusting, punte, drill with a high thrust and cover followed by a low thrust and cover before swapping. Alternatively as a variation on our sword exercise drill where the low opportunistic cut is countered by a cut to the head – which does not land for training – to demonstrate the counter to this cut when it is not opportunistically available.

Sword Cover Drill

In principle this is a very simple drill, but it can be very demanding.

One training partner (Green) cuts with a Fendente from the right and the other partner (Red) then performs an Inside Sword Cover. The attacker (Green) then cuts with a Fendente from the left and the other partner (Red) performs an Outside Sword Cover

The two training partners then swap – with Red first attacking Green with a Fendente from the right, which Green counters with an Inside Sword Cover, followed by Red attacking with a Fendente from the left with Green performing an Outside Sword Cover. The partners then swap moves again and the drill continues.

This is also an important movement drill as each combination of attack and cover will require that the training partners continually adjust their positions. Such footwork is important and needs to be incorporated within this drill.

Sword Beat Drill

The sword beat drill should be performed as a regular flow from one side to the other.

In this example, Red beats Green's Fendente, from the right, with an Outside Beat. Green then re-adjusts and cuts with a Fendente from the left. Red has also re-adjusted, low to the right, and performs and Inside Beat.

Once this combination has taken place Red and Green will swap, with Red performing the Fendente cuts from the right and the left against which Green will Beat from the Inside and the Outside. Then they will swap and the drill will continue.

This drill should flow back and forward with each training partner performing two Beats before swapping to attack the other partner with two Fendentes. Footwork should also flow naturally with the drill allowing the training partners to come around each other during the drill.

Sword Break Drill

Drilling with Sword Breaks needs to be done under a lot more control due to the nature of the power used with the technique. For this reason this drill should be more of a walk-through rather than a built-up flow drill.

Initially Green attacks with a Mezani from the right, against which Red steps in with an Inside Break. Green then cuts around to perform a false-edge Mezani from the left, against which Red performs an Outside Break. The two training partners then swap, with Red performing the Mezani cuts and Green the breaks, before swapping again – and so on.

Sword Exercise Drill

This is a simple drill that is very good for conditioning, when used with repetition, where each Player will perform the same actions as the other. This is a cooperative drill where the swords are intended to meet on the cuts.

Both Players start in the same position with their swords high to the right and left foot forward. ▲

Both Players perform a Fendente cut from the right, stepping off line with a Mezza Volta. The swords meet. This practises a normal Fendente cut from the right with correct footwork. ◀

Both Players accrease (see footwork) to their left and start a Tutta Volta, wielding their swords around ready for a Fendente from the left. This practises both footwork and coming around to the left of an opponent. ▶

Sword Exercise Drill

(Continued from previous page)

The Tutta Voltas are completed with each Player doing a Fendente cut from the left. The swords meet. This practises a normal Fendente cut from the left with footwork.

Both Players accrease to their right and start a Tutta Volta, wielding their swords around ready for a Fendente from the right. This practises both footwork and coming around to the right of an opponent.

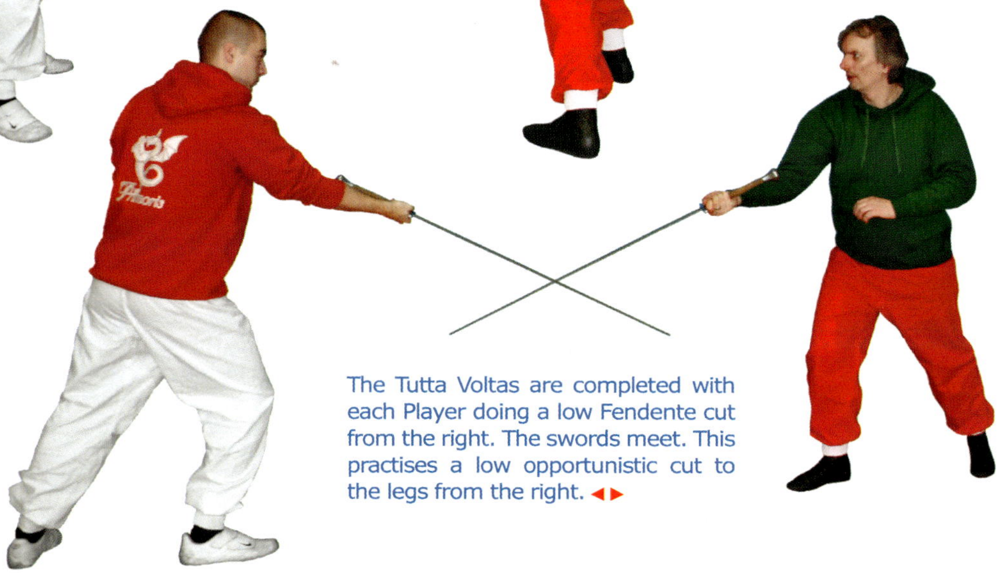

The Tutta Voltas are completed with each Player doing a low Fendente cut from the right. The swords meet. This practises a low opportunistic cut to the legs from the right.

Sword Exercise Drill

(Continued from previous page)

Both players accrease to their left and start a Tutta Volta, wielding their swords around ready for a Fendente from the left. This practises both footwork and coming around to the left of an opponent. ►

The Tutta Voltas are completed with each Player doing a low Fendente cut from the left. The swords meet. This practises a low opportunistic cut to the legs from the left. ◄►

The Players now withdraw their swords ready for a Punte thrust. This practises the withdrawal of the sword with weight adjustment and the preparation for a thrust. ◄►

Sword Exercise Drill

(Continued from previous page)

Each Player now does a Punte thrust at the other with a Mezza Volta. The incoming thrust is deflected offline with the back of the hand. This practises both thrusts with footwork and the principle of deflection which is expanded upon in later levels. ◄

The Players now recover their swords with a left side Cover and withdraw the leading right leg. This practises recovery under a Cover and the protection of the leading leg by simple withdrawal. ◄►

Each Player now does a quick Fendente cut from the left, avoiding the other Player for safety. This practises the quick counter cut from a Cover. ►

The Players now reset to the starting position and the drill is repeated. Normally this drill should be repeated between 10 and 20 times. As confidence and speed builds the footwork should bring each Player more off line. It is important that both Players work together to get the tempo of the drill correct, which is also a good physical exercise.

Historical Reference

As part of Primoris training it is important that you understand and appreciate the original martial basis behind the system of Fiore. This section gives some relevant original manuscript reference that both relates to the Primoris training and gives an historical background. This is just an extract from one of the manuscripts and later levels will expand upon this reference base as the training increases and expands.

This text is archaic but you should try to understand as much as possible. For example, the introduction presents the Masters of Fiore, together with other key martial elements; helping to maintain the bridge between the modern and historical practitioners.

Do not expect to see everything here, as the manuscripts assumed a lot of basic knowledge that is now taught within Primoris and later levels.

Manuscript Introduction

Fior Furlan de Civida of Austria that is of Messr Benedetto of the noble family of liberi from Premariacco of the diocese of the Patriarch of Aquilegia, in his youth he wanted to learn of armed fighting and the art of combat in the barriers.

Of spear, axe, sword and dagger and of unarmed on foot and on horse in armour and without armour. Also he wanted to understand the temper of iron.

And features of each weapon as well as to defend when to attack and most of all of the fight to the death

Also other wonderful and secret things which are evident to few men of the world.

And they are truest and of greatest offence and of large defence and things that he cannot fail as they are so easy to do.

Which art and teaching that is said before.

And the said Fiore learned these things from many German Masters.

And from many Italians in more provinces and in many of the largest cities and with great expenses.

And for the grace of God from many Masters and Scholars.

And in the courts of great gentlemen, Princes, Dukes, Marquises and Counts, Knights and Squires he learned much of this Art.

That the said Fiore was more and more times required by many Gentleman and Knights and Squires for learning from the said Fiore made art of all arms and armour and fighting in the barriers to the death which art he has demonstrated to more Italian and German and other great Gentleman who had to fight in the barriers.

And also of countless others that did not have to fight.

And of some that have been at times my Scholars who had to fight in the barriers.

Of which some I will make name and remember here.

First of them I know, the noble and strong Knight Sir Piero del Verde who had to fight with Sir Piero de la Corona who were both German.

And the battle was held in Perosa.

Also to the valiant Knight Sir Nicolo Voriçilino a German that had to fight with Nicolo Inghileso. The field was set at Imola.

Also to the notable, valiant and strong knight Sir Galeaço the Captain of Grimello called from Mantoa that had to fight with the valiant knight Sir Buçichardo of France in the field of Padoa.

Also to the valiant squire Lancilotto da Becharia of Pavia and he made 6 thrusts with the lance of soft iron on horseback against the knight Sir Baldassaro, a German, who had to, in Imola, fight in the barriers.

Also to the valiant squire çoanino da Bavo from Milan who made, in Pavia, in the castle, against the valiant German squire Sram, three thrusts of the lance of soft iron on horseback.

And then he made on foot three blows of axe and three blows of sword and three blows of dagger in the presence of the noblest prince and Lord Sir the Duke of Milan and the Lady Duchess and other countless Gentlemen and Ladies.

Also to the cautious knight Sir Açço da Castell Barcho that once had to fight with Çuanne di Ordelaffi.

And another time with the valiant and good knight Sir Jacomo di Boson and the field had to be to the pleasure of the Lord Duke of Milan, of these and of others that I, Fiore, have taught I am very content because I have been well rewarded and I have held the honour and the love of my scholars and their relatives.

I say also that this art I have demonstrated it always in secret so that not anyone stood present at the demonstration except the Scholar and discreet relatives, and also if anyone other they stayed for grace or for courtesy, with holy vows they pledge a promise in faith not to reveal to anyone the plays they saw from me Master Fiore.

And mostly I have been wary of Fencing Masters and of their Scholars. And they with envy namely these Masters demanded me to play with swords with cut and with thrust in an arming doublet without other armour but a pair of gloves of chamois and all this is because I did not want to practice with them nor did I want to teach them anything of my art.

And this accident happened 5 times that I have been required.

Manuscript Introduction

And 5 times for my honour I met them, I played in strange places without relatives and without friends not having hope in anyone but in God, in the Art and myself, Fiore, and in my sword.

And with the grace of God I, Fiore, remained with honour and without lesions to my person.

Also I, Fiore, said to my Scholars who had to fight in the barriers that fighting in the barriers is of much (much) less danger than fighting with swords of cut and of thrust in arming doublets because in plays with sharp swords one single cover that fails in that blow gives him death.

And one that fights in the barriers and is well armoured he can receive strikes. Yet still he can gain victory of the fight.

Also it is another thing that rarely has any one perished because they had been taken by surprise.

So that I say that I would rather fight three times in the barriers than one single time with sharp swords like well I said.

And thus I say that the one that fights in the barriers being well armoured, and knowing the art of fighting and having the advantages that if he can be taken, if he is not of any worth he shall be very willing to hang himself, well that I can say for the grace of God that not one of my scholars has not lost in this art. Rather they have always remained with honour.

Also say I, aforementioned Fiore, that these gentlemen, knights and squires to whom I showed this art of combat, they have been satisfied with my teaching not wanting other than me for master.

Also I say that not one of my scholars in particular those mentioned above, have had a book about the art of combat other than Sir Galeazo da Mantoa.

Well that he said that without books no one shall be a good Master nor Scholar in this art.

And I, Fiore, confirm it true that this art is long that there is no man of the world of great memory that he can hold in mind without books a quarter part of this art.

Given that not knowing more than a quarter part of this art I shall not be a Master.

That I, Fiore, knowing how to read and to write and to draw and having books in this art and I have studied for 40 years or more. Also I am not a very perfect Master in this art. Although it is held by great gentlemen, who have at times been my scholars, I am a good and perfect Master in the mentioned art.

And if I say that I had studied for 40 years in law, in politics and in medicine like I have studied in the art of arms then I would be a doctor in those three sciences.

And in this science of arms I have had large contention with fatigue and expense to be even a good Scholar we say of other things.

Considering I, the aforementioned Fiore, that in this art I would find few Masters in the world and wanting to make a memory of me I will make a book in all the art and of all that which I know and of iron and of temper and other things following the order which my high Gentleman says, who is above others for martial virtue, prefers me more and more deserving of this my book for his nobility than other Gentleman that I may see and I could see, that is my illustrious and excellent powerful Lord Prince Sir Nicolo Marquis of Este, Lord of the noble city of Ferara of Modena. Reço of Parma etc. to who God gives good life and future prosperity with victory over his enemies. AMEN.

Let us start the book following the order of my Lord Marquis and we fashion it so that he does not lack for nothing in the art that I yield; I count that my Lord will make good merit to me due to his great nobility and courtesy.

And let us start with Abraçare, which is done for two reasons, which is for sport and for anger, that is for life with every guile and deceit and cruelty that he can do.

And of this that I do for life I want to speak and to show with reason and most of all gaining holds that are used when you are fighting for life.

The man that wants to do Abraçare wants to be advised about he who he will fight with if the companion is stronger or if he is big of the body and if he younger or older.

Also he wants to see if he uses the guards of Abraçare and of all these things is to be foreseen.

And nothing less he puts himself always stronger or less strong in the prese of the ligadure and always defends from the prese of his opponent.

And if your enemy is unarmoured wait to hurt him in those places more grievous and more hazardous, which are in his eyes, the nose, in the soft under the chin and in the flanks. And nothing less, watch if he can come to you with the prese or the ligadure, armoured or unarmoured, so that it was one and the other.

Also I say that to Abraçare wants to have 8 things called strength, speed, knowledge, namely to know the advantageous prese, knowledge to make breaks namely break arms and legs, to know ligadure namely binds of arms in this way that a man does not have more defence and he cannot move freely, to know how to hurt in the hazardous places.

Also know to put one to ground without danger to himself.

Also knowing of dislocating arms and legs in various ways.

Of which all things I write and I will draw in this book, step by step, as the art requires.

We have said that which Abraçare requires now we speak of the guards of Abraçare.

The guards of Abraçare can be done in various ways and one way is better than the other.

But these 4 guards are best in armour and without armour, however the guards do not have firmness for the sudden prese that he does.

The first 4 Masters that you see with the crowns on their head for those show the guards of Abraçare called Posta Longa and Dente di Cengiaro that makes one the contrary of the other and then can make Porta di Ferro and Posta Frontale the one in contrary to the other.

And these four guards can do all those things said before about Abraçare in armour and without armour namely the prese and the ligadure and breaks etc.

Even as it must be made in the way that the guards themselves are known by the Master Players and the Scholars from the Players and the Players from Masters and the Remedy of the good Contrary that always the Contrary is placed after the Remedy and sometimes the Remedy is after, or after all of his Plays and this we will make clear.

We say that knowing the guards or posta is easy. First that the guards have their arms in hand the one against the other and is not touching one with the other.

And they stand heedfully and firm one against the other in order to see that which the companion wants to do.

And these are called poste or guards or the First Masters of Battle.

And these wear a crown on the head because they are positioned in a place and in this way can make great defence with such an position.

And they are the principles of this art that is of that art of arms with which the said Master remain in guard.

And so much is to say that posta is guard.

And guard is a lot to say that the man guards himself and defends himself from the wounds from his enemy.

And so much is to say that posta is the way of positioning his enemy in order to offend him without danger to oneself.

The other Masters that follow the four guards descend from the guards and comes to defend himself from another Player with the blows that are of the four guards who are before. And this Master wears also a crown, and he is called second master.

Also he is called Master Remedy because he does the remedy that are not receiving of wounds or that are not carelessly made in this art that are the said poste or guards.

And this second one, called Remedy has players under himself who play those plays that are played by the Master that is called Remedy taking this cover or Presa that is done by the said Remedy. And these Players wear a device under the knee. And these Players do all of the Plays of the Remedy until such that they find another Master that will make the Contrary of the Remedy and of all his Players.

And because he makes Contrary to the Remedy and Contrary to his Players he will wear the device of Master Remedy and his Players namely the crown on the head and the device under the knee and this King is called Third Master and he is called Contrary because he will be against the other Masters and against his Plays.

Also I say that in some places in the art the Fourth Master, called King, is found who will do the contrary of the Third King, called the Contrary of the Remedy. And this King is the Fourth Master called Fourth Master.

And he is called Contra-contrary.

Manuscript Introduction

Although few plays pass the Third Master in the art.

And the more he does this he does with danger. And I have said enough of this.

As we have spoken here before of the guards of Abrazare and the Second Master that is of the Remedy and of his Players and of the Third Master Contrary to the Second Master and his Players, and of the Fourth Master that is called Contra-contrary, so as these Masters and Players have to conduct the art of Abrazare in armour and without armour and these Masters and Players have to conduct the art of the lance with lance and those guards, Masters and Players.

And in a similar way with the axe and with the sword of one hand and of two hands. And in a similar way with the dagger.

So that for effect these Masters and Players mentioned before, with their standards and devices, have to conduct all the art of armed combat on foot and from horse in armour and without armour.

Following as they do in the plays of Abrazare.

And this only means that it must be like this, guards and Masters in the other arts and Remedy and Contrary like in the art of Abrazare so that the book can be easily understood.

Although the inscriptions and the figures and the plays show all the art so well that all should be understood.

Now we attend to the drawn figures and to their plays and to their words which will show the truth.

Abrazare Posta

I am posta longa and like this you look. And in the presa that you wish to do to me, my right arm that is raised, I will place it under your left for certain. And I enter in the first play of Abrazare, and with such presa I will make you go to ground. And if that presa was likely to fail me, to the other prese that follow I know to enter.

In dente di zenghiar against you I come. I am sure to break your presa with my hold. And from this I leave and to porta di ferro I enter. And in order to put you to ground I will be prepared. And if this that I said fails me because of your defence I will search for other ways of making offence to you, namely with breaks, binds and dislocations. In that way that is written in the figures.

Abrazare Posta

In porta di ferro I wait for you without movement in order to earn the presa with all my own ability. The play of Abrazare by that is my art. And of Spear, Axe, Sword and dagger a great part. Porta di ferro is with malice filled. Who counters me I always give contention and pain. And to you that counters me then the presa I earn, with the strong presa I will make you go to ground.

I am posta frontale in order to earn the prese. Those who come at me in this position, you make offense. But I will move from this guard. And with knowing I will move you from porta di ferro. Then I will make you stand [so] that you would abide in hell. Of binding and breaking I will do easily to you. And soon he will be looking at those I have earned. And the prese I will earn if I will not be forgotten.

Daga Posta

I am Full Iron Door and I am single. And I am good in armour and without, because I can beat and I do with presa and without, and I can play with the dagger and without and I make my covers.

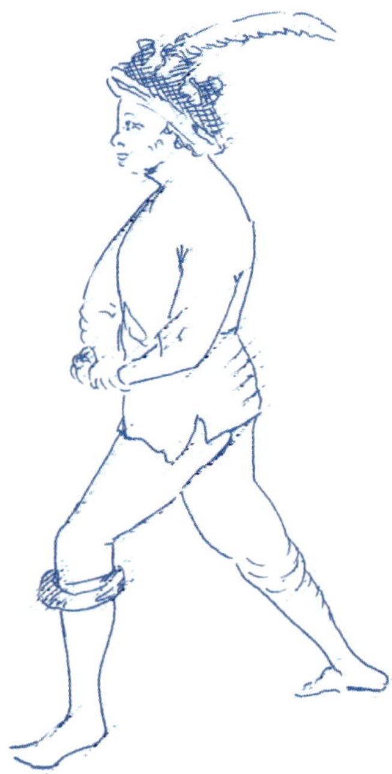

I am Full Iron Door and I am double, and I am good in armour and without, and also I am better in armour than without, and with such a guard I cannot use a dagger.

Daga Posta

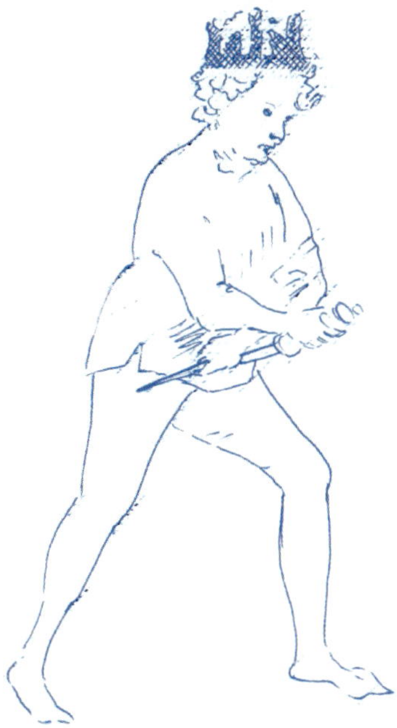

And I am Middle Iron Door and I am double crossed. And I am good in armour and not without because I cannot make long covers and I can cover high and low with the right hand and with the left hand with dagger and without.

I am Middle Iron Door with the dagger in hand and I am double and better and more strong then all the others and I am good in armour and without and I can cover high and low and every side.

And I am Full Iron Door with the arms crossed and I am double and I am in a strong position and in armour I am good and strong. And without armour I am not sufficient because I cannot cover long.

Daga Blows

Of the dangerous knife that of everything I doubt, the arms, the hands and the two elbows quickly go against it. And I shall do these five things always. Namely I take the dagger and strike, I break the arms and I bind them and I force him to ground. And if of these five plays one or the other I will not abandon. He who knows to defend himself guards the body.

With downward blows I can hurt the head and the body from the elbow ending at the top of the head. And from the elbow down I do not have sure freedom without much danger, and of this strike I have doubts.

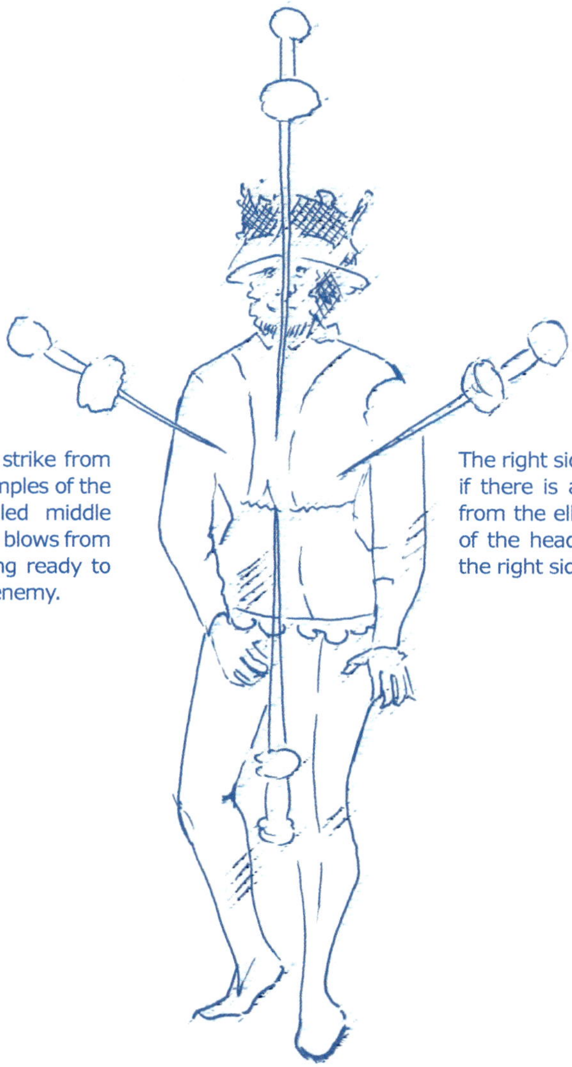

From the left side he can strike from the elbow to end at the temples of the head. And they are called middle (mezani) blows. And those blows from the left he cannot do being ready to make a cover against his enemy.

The right side can strike and can cover if there is a need, and he can strike from the elbow to end at the temples of the head, and more assured from the right side [than] that of the left.

The dagger that goes through the middle towards your head he can strike to end under the chest and not higher and always with the left hand he can cover.

I am the noble weapon that is called dagger that is of the Close Play, I am very moving and restless. And he who knows my malice and my art of every subtle [weapon] fight will have a good part. And to end suddenly my fierce battle there is not a man that can go against me. And he who sees me in a feat of arms, covers and thrusts I shall do with it, abrazare, and remove his dagger with breaks and binds. And against me neither arms nor armour are to be of value.

Requisites of Daga

Because I carry the dagger in my right hand I carry it for my art that she has well deserved, that anyone that draws a dagger to me, I will take it from his hand, and with that I know well to injure, because of the pros and cons of all endings.

For his broken arms that I carry, I want to say my art, because this is without wanting to lie, that I have not broken and dislocated in my life, and he who will put himself against my art I want to make, such art always I am ready to want to use.

Requisites of Daga

I am the Master of Opening, and also of Holding namely the arms of those who want to fight against me. I want to put him in large trouble and suffering in the ways that the binds and breaks are drawn. And because I carry the key for a standard that such art is very worthy to me.

They ask me, why I hold this man under my feet, because I have no better place with such a finish with the art of Abrazare. And for Victory I carry the Palm in the right hand because with Abrazare he knows he will never remain.

Daga Master Remedies

I am the First Master and called Remedy, because that great remedy is to say that I know to remedy so that you cannot strike me, and that I might strike and injure your contrary enemy.

For this he cannot do better, your dagger I will make go to earth, turning my hand to the left side.

I play with the arms crossed as I am about to do the remedies that have passed before. And if we were both armoured we would not think of making a better cover. A more stronger remedy than me does not wear a crown, because I can play to the right and the left, also I can cross below like above.

Here begins the plays of the other hand for which countless men have lost their lives. And the plays of my students will follow also for the covers which I fashion with the right hand.

This is a simple play to do in this way that I will want to throw him to the ground.

Daga Master Remedies

I am the fourth Master who plays with this presa. With similar to this my scholars will offend many. And if I turn to the right side and I do not release your arm, I will take your dagger and I will make trouble for you with it.

I am the Fifth Master King for the collar hold of this player. That before he draws his dagger on me, in this way I break his arm, because the hold with which he holds me is of great advantage to me. Because I can do all the covers, prese and binds of all the other master remedies and of their scholars who are before. The proverb speaks for an example. I want that everyone that has a scholar in this art knows that taking the presa of the collar nobody can defend without speed.

I am the Sixth Master that says that this cover is fine in armour and without armour. And with such a cover I can cover every side, and enter into all binds and do prese and to strike according to what my scholars will follow unto the end. And this cover is fashioned by everyone of my scholars, And they can do those plays that they can possibly do after that.

Daga Master Remedies

I am the Seventh Master that plays with the arms crossed, and this cover is worth more in armour than without armour. That with such a cover I can do the plays that came before, namely the middle bind that is the third play of the first master remedy of dagger. Also I can make you turn grabbing with my left hand your right elbow. And I can immediately strike you in the head or the shoulders. And this cover is more useful for binding than doing anything else, and it is the strongest cover against the dagger.

I am the Eighth Master and I cross with my dagger. And this play is good in armour and without armour. And some of my plays are placed before and some after. The play that is before me which is the fourth play namely that I strike the player in the hand with the point of his dagger, in a similar way I can strike the hand from below like he can strike from above. Also I can take his hand in the joint with my left hand and with the right I can injure him then you will find me as the ninth scholar of the ninth master that strikes the player in the chest. Also I can do last play if I have abandoned my dagger.

I am the ninth King and I am not of the dagger any more and this prese that I make underneath resembles the prese done by the Fourth King from above the hand as I do from under. But my plays cannot be done with nought And this presa is good in armour and without because I can make a lot of plays. And most of all those that follow me. In armour and without of them there is not a doubt.

Spada Una Mano

We are three Players that intend to kill this Master. One will throw the point (thrust), the other with a cut, the other wants to throw his sword against the said Master. So that it will be a very great fact he is not dead that God makes him very sorrowful.

You have bad desires and of this art you know little. You do things that have no place in words. Come one by one who knows how to do it and even if you were one hundred I will put you all out of order because of this guard that is so good and strong. I accrease the foot that is forward a little out of the way and with the left I pass to the side (traverse). And in that pass I cross beating the sword to you I find you revealed and of wounding you I will make certain. And if a spear or sword is thrown at me, I will beat them all like I have said passing out of the way. As you will see in my plays that follow here after, I pray that you look at them. And even with a one handed sword I will do my art as it is after in these papers.

Seven Colpi

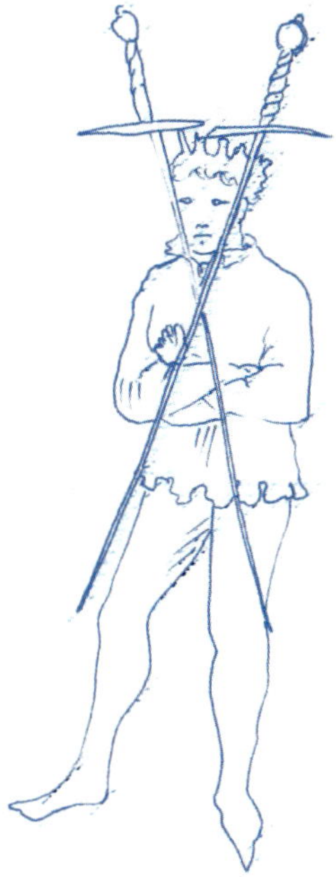

We are Fendente and in the art we make issue of cleaving from the teeth and to arrive at the knee with reason. And every guard who makes itself low to the ground, from one guard to another we go without trouble. And we break the guards with cunning and with blows we make the blood sign. We fendente will not wait to strike, and we return to guard from passage to passage.

The Sottani blows are we, and we start at the knee, and we go through the middle of the forehead through the path made by the fendente. And in this way we are both together for by that path we return, or that we remain in Posta Longa.

Seven Colpi

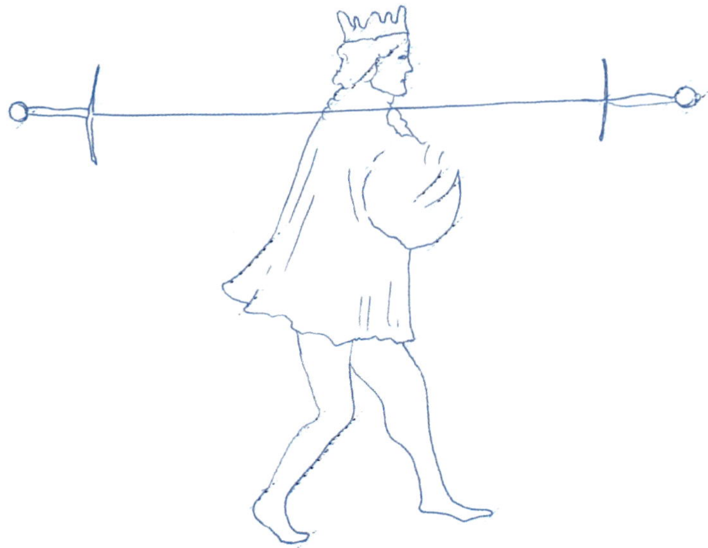

Mezani blows we are called because we go through the middle of the high and low blows. And we go with the right edge from the right side, and from the opposite side we go with the false edge. And our path is from the knees to the head.

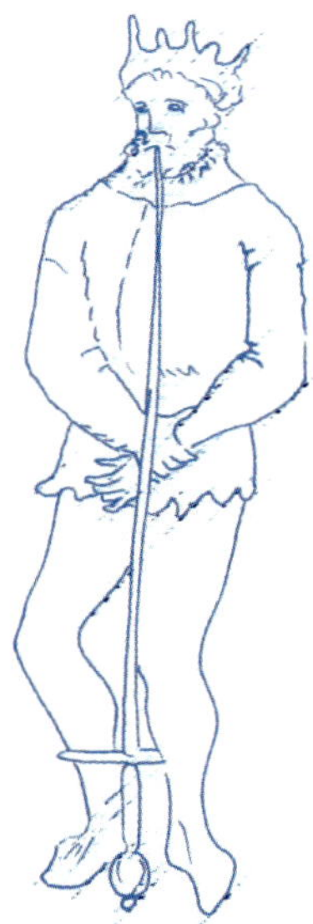

We are the Punte cruel and deadly. And our path is through the middle of the body beginning at the pubic region to the forehead. And we thrust with five reasons, namely two high one on one side and the other from the other. And two from low similarly one from one side and the other from the other side, and one from the middle that is from Middle Iron Door or from Posta Longa and Posta Breve.

Segno

This Master with these swords signifies the seven blows of the sword. And the four animals signify four virtues, namely advise, quickness, strength, and daring. And he who wants to be good in this art from these virtues together they will have their part.

Advisement

Better than me, the lynx, no creature sees. And by that I always place with compass and measure.

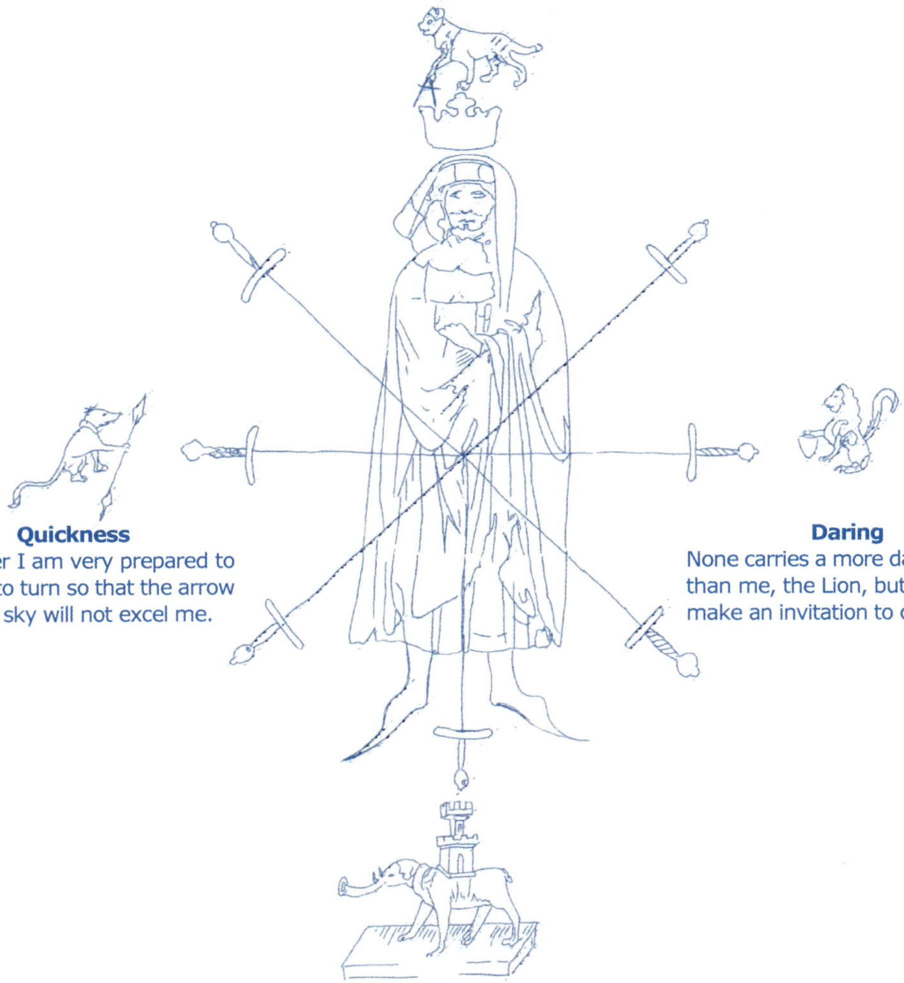

Quickness

I am tiger I am very prepared to run and to turn so that the arrow from the sky will not excel me.

Daring

None carries a more daring heart than me, the Lion, but of battle I make an invitation to others.

Strength

Elephant I am and a castle I carry for a load. And I do not kneel nor lose balance.

Glossary of Italian Terms

Abrazare
Unarmed Combat, combines elements of both grappling and striking. Literal translation "with arms".

Azza
Axe - refers to Pollaxe

Colpi
Blows, as in strikes.

Colpi Fendente
Downward blows. In Fiore's system these blows take the path from the teeth to the knees at an oblique angle.

Colpi Mezani
Middle/horizontal blows. These are done with the True Edge leading from the right and the false edge leading from the left.

Colpi Sottani
Upward blows. Normally done with the false edge, enabling a quick return with a fendente, but true edge application should not be ignored.

Coverta
Cover. An action that covers a line of attack enabling the Scholar to move safely behind it to a better position.

Daga
Dagger. The dagger used in Fiore's texts is a rondel with no discernible edge, therefore most techniques are designed to finish with a stab, not a cut.

Fendente
Downward cleaving blow.

Gioco Largo
Wide, loose play - done at distance.

Gioco Stretto
Tight, narrow play. A used to describe technique where the Scholar enters to a close range to seize and grapple the Player or his weapon.

Guardia
A guard which guards against an attack. Not the same as Posta as Posta is a position that guards and attacks simultaneously. Having said that the term is sometimes used interchangeably with Posta.

Lanza
Spear, when on foot, Lance when on horse.

Ligadura Mezana
Middle Bind.

Ligadura Soprana
High Bind.

Ligadura di Sotto/Ligadura Sottana
Under Bind.

Mezza Volta
Half Turn. Essentially refers to passing footwork, enabling the Scholar to fight on both sides, in front and behind.

Posta
Position; a position that is adopted which simultaneously defends from attacks and threatens attacks. A sentinel position of readiness.

Pui Fortezza
More Strength - a technique described as a dagger defence from the First Master Remedy of Dagger to provide the cover with more strength against an attack.

Prese
A hold, take or catch. The term is used slightly differently depending on the context in which it is employed.

Punte/Punta/Punto
Thrust or Point depending on context.

Rebattere
Beat. An action of beating back an attack, usually taking the form of cutting under the opposing weapon and knocking it back towards the Player.

Spada
Sword

Spada a una mano
Sword used with one hand.

Spada a due mani
Sword used with two hands.

Tagli
Cut or Slice.

Tutta Volta
Full/Complete Turn. Footwork where one foot turns about the other in a circular motion.

Volta Stabile
Stable Turn. Footwork where the Scholar turns on the balls of their feet to face the opposite direction. Enables the Scholar to fight in front, behind and to one side.

Moving Forward

Now that you have completed the Primoris training programme you will be looking to see where you can go next. There are several options available to you. You can continue our training programme by moving onto Secundus; you can formalise your own training; you could join a Martial Arts School.

This section is intended to give you some ideas and pointers. The Martial Arts community is very large and a lot of people will be willing to give help and advice - do not be afraid to ask.

With attention to the Health and Safety aspects of Primoris you can use this training programme for sparring and free play, but always remember that this is something that you should build up to.

Finally, you can come to The Exiles for formal training and grading.

Lesson Planning

If you are looking at creating formal training around Primoris then it is a good idea to create lesson plans. These will allow you to build up the training and keep a formal record as students progress. The following is an example lesson plan that you may use as a template – it may be a lesson in itself or form part of a larger lesson.

Remember that lesson planning should be based around good Health and Safety. This means that you should know the students and maintain all of the basic Health and Safety requirements - medical kit; accident book; insurance; etc.

Do not take on formal training without serious thought. It is very easy to set up a Martial Arts School and make grand claims, but it is a lot more difficult to become a good martial artist first.

If you are just planning on study training then it is still a good idea to have a lesson plan as this will let you monitor your training over time.

Example Lesson Plan

LESSON: ONE HANDED OUTSIDE SWORD BEATS

Type of Activity: *Solo or Group*

Handouts: *Notes on One Handed Outside Sword Beats*

Equipment: *Sword, Mask, Gloves*

Aims

- Introduce the Student to the concept of Beats as a defence
- Introduce the concept that the Beat is the same as the Sottani
- Show connection with Fendente
- Consolidate knowledge on footwork and turning
- Use the Outside Beat to show the concepts of zoning and exploitation of outside line consolidated
- Introduce Outside Beat Practice

Assumed K owledge *Students should know*

- Names, lines and directions of the cuts of Fiore
- Footwork, names, lines of movement
- Unarmed Posta
- Concepts of zoning and exploitation of outside line

Lesson

1) Explain to Students what a Beat is:

- Sottani Cut
- Defensive movement against sword
- Aggressive defence against opponent's arm

2) Show Outside Beat in action. Draw attention to foot work and the offline movements
3) Get students in pairs to try the action
4) Go through the main points of the technique:

- Explain that the line of the Beat follows that of a Sottani
- Show that this is the same line that the Fendente comes down
- Tell Students that always after a Sottani they will be ready with a Fendente and vice versa
- Show Outside Beat followed by Fendente attack
- Draw attention to the footwork and positioning of body before Beat, after Beat, before Fendente, and after Fendente

5) Students try technique
6) Explain and show to students zoning aspects, distance aspects, and different targets
7) Build into a simple drill. Single Cut, with Beat reply

Assessment

- Pay attention to Student's footwork, ensure that proper line is being gained
- Pay attention to the Sottani cut performing Beat
- Ensure that the Student is cutting straight with appropriate arm and wrist movement
- Ensure that Student is not turning wrist to try and come over the opponent's sword with the false edge
- Pay attention to end position of Student in relation to opponent

Conclusion

- Reiterate salient points from lesson
- Feedback on class in general and individuals specifically - ONLY POSITIVE
- POINTS
- Negative issues should be pointed out during the lesson to individuals only
- Remind Students of common mistakes that should be avoided
- Show Students where and how this will be developed in next lesson
- Show Students how the lesson will be connected to demonstrating Covers in future lessons

Grading

If, having completed your Primoris training, you wish to be graded then you can approach The Exiles for formal grading. This training programme forms the first part of the entire Exiles training programme and each level requires a grading step.

As part of the grading you will be assessed as to your knowledge of the Primoris material and how you apply this knowledge in practice.

This is a formal assessment and is expected of all students that train with The Exiles before they are allowed to move onto the next stage of training. As a student progresses through the curriculum they need to be focused on a specific set of goals, so with each new level a new layer of skills is built upon previous levels.

Choosing to be graded is a personal choice and may not be practical due to distance, but The Exiles have opened up this grading process to accompany the release of Primoris so that the option is available.

If you would like to be graded then please contact The Exiles Secretary - secretary@the-exiles.org.uk

You may find that the Primoris programme also fits into the grading structures of other Martial Arts Schools and it is worth approaching such schools if you are unable to attend Exiles grading.

Exiles Grading

It is neither possible nor correct to fully outline the grading process. The full grading contains many items which are designed to examine the student's knowledge and experience.

Within The Exiles a student will normally go for their grading after 13 to 16 weeks on the Primoris programme.

This diagram shows the five elements that are looked for during the grading. Each has equal importance and all of the information is contained within this Primoris programme.

The grading does not look for martial perfection from Primoris, but rather a martial understanding that can be built upon within Secundus. The grading process itself is deliberately intense and lasts about two hours. This builds up a level of tiredness that helps to demonstrate the unconscious knowledge that student has learned.

It may appear strange that Health and Safety is equal to, say, Unarmed but this covers more than just basic Health and Safety knowledge. The student must demonstrate a practical consideration for Health and Safety during the Unarmed aspect of the grading - for example, tapping out; acknowledging a tap out from a training partner; throwing a partner safely; knowing how to fall safely, etc.

In the same way Theory covers martial application and historical theory that are both relevant to the subject.

Sparring

Sparring is a form of free fighting with rules and regulations. The level of rules and regulations determine the style and free play level of the sparring.

When used correctly sparring is an excellent training tool that can build upon the techniques that you have learned and expose weakness.

If you have a trusted training partner and a good understanding of Health and Safety then sparring can become a very enjoyable and intense goal for your training. You must, however, always remember the Health and Safety aspects and ensure that those sparring do so at an equal level.

When you start sparring you should always wear protection. If you get to a high level of competence, rather than just confidence, then you can reduce the protection and replace it with good awareness and understanding between the two sparring partners. Never, though, move onto complete free form sparring without complete protection.

You can spar at half speed; using only certain lines of attack or defence; to the first strike; etc.

Adapt your sparring to your training so that it becomes an extension to increase your skill level. Do not rush as this will introduce bad habits.

Sparring

In this example of sparring, within training, the partners have agreed that Green will only use high attacks. Green is competent enough to redirect or pull his attack if necessary, but still uses a wooden waster rondel.

Red is able to practise Dagger Master techniques at full speed, whilst Green is able to practise both attacking and falling safely. Note that Red also controls his techniques so that he does not actually damage Green's arm.

Resources

Primoris is more than just a book - it also has a DVD and reference material. You can use this to expand upon your Primoris training and move onto the Secundus training programme.

There are, however, several other resources available to you. Most of these can be accessed directly via the Internet and we would encourage you to actively contact other Martial Arts communities and schools.

Any form of Martial Arts training requires the correct equipment and we have listed an example of some good suppliers.

Do not take this section as being an exhaustive list, rather use this as a basis for your own study and find out what is available.

Remember that if in doubt then ask.

Continued Curriculum

One of the objectives of Primoris is to introduce students to a formalised training programme. This is not completely possible within a book and so we offer a lot more support and help.

A DVD is available to accompany this book. Together these give the full picture of the training material - reference and action. In addition to this we have a Fiore dei Liberi reference book that provides the original source material behind the entire art.

You can come on-line to The Exiles web site - www.the-exiles.org.uk - where there is more information available; a shop for equipment and material and a discussion forum.

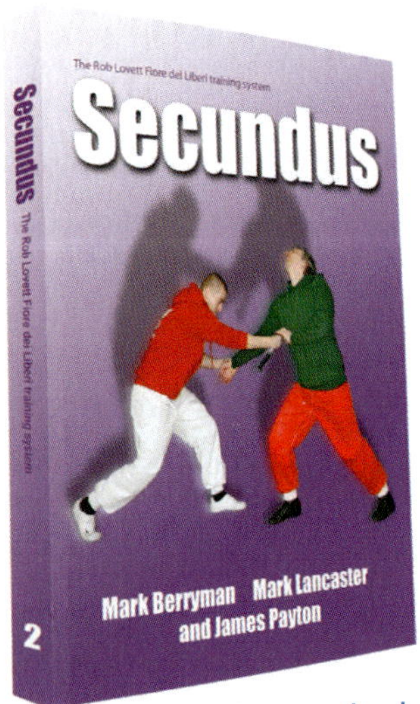

The Exiles would also welcome you to training as well, or maybe you would just like to come to workshops or apply for grading on your own Primoris training.

However you decide to continue there is a lot help and advice available.

We would hope that you would decide to stay with our curriculum and move onto the next stage. Secundus expands upon the topics covered within Primoris and introduces the sword in two hands. This is all part of a curriculum build up to ensure that you have the best information available at each stage of training.

The Exiles also run study groups called ESGs (Exiles Study Group). These can be either practice groups in different locations and countries or they can be research groups. Research groups focus on different areas of this large subject - for example the history behind Fiore dei Liberi. Practice groups can be formed to allow for a recognised approach to the curriculum.

If you want more information or have any questions on how to move forward within this curriculum then please contact The Exiles Secretary - secretary@ he-exiles.org.uk

Online Resources

Discussion Forums

www.the-exiles.org.uk/forum
This is the on-line discussion forum for The Exiles. You can discuss general topics or specific Primoris topics.

www.bfhs.co.uk/html/phpBB3
The public discussion forum of the UK BFHS, an umbrella organisation for UK based Historical European Martial Arts Schools.

www.swordforum.com
Sword Forum is an international discussion forum on any subject related to swords. There are specific areas with discussions on Historical European Martial Arts.

www.fioredeiliberi.org/phpBB3
The Schola Swordmanship Forum has a specific Fiore dei Liberi discussion area as well as wider discussions on Historical European Martial Arts.

www.martialartsplanet.com/forums
A general Martial Arts forum that also has a discussion area on Western Martial Arts.

Equipment Suppliers

www.thatguysproducts.com
Specialist masks and gorget protection designed specifically for Historical European Martial Arts.

www.albion-swords.com
Sword supplier that includes the Maestro range of sparring swords.

www.lutel.cz
Suppliers of Rondel Daggers and other period weaponry.

www.the-exiles.org.uk
The Exiles supply Rondel training wasters via their on-line shop.

www.revival.us
In addition to general period items, Revival supply sparring hand protection, gorgets and head protection together with safety training weapons.

shop.suspensionofdisbelief.co.uk/hema
The Grange runs a specialist shop providing both training weapons and safety equipment, as well as books and DVDs.

www.theknightshop.co.uk
A UK supplier of period items that includes specialist protection equipment and a good range of nylon sword wasters.

www.leonpaul.co.uk
Suppliers of Fencing Equipment, including 1600N masks, mask covers and Jackets.

www.allstar.de
Suppliers of Fencing Equipment, including Master Jackets, mask covers and 1600N masks.

Primoris

www.primoristraining.com
The Primoris main web link for information and details on the entire training programme.

Index

Index